Contents

Plates

Maps

Genealogical Tables

Preface

The Normans have been the subject of many books, from the Middle Ages onwards. One of their characteristic traits was a love of hearing the history of their heroes and their achievements; some of the earliest chronicles dealing with these topics have survived and been published. Modern historians have carried on the tradition in a more critical spirit. Among the pioneers were C. H. Haskins at Harvard and E. M. Jamison at Oxford, who looked at the various aspects of their civilization and the institutions in the countries where they settled. More recently D. C. Douglas and R. Allen Brown, Lucien Musset and many others have written at length of their achievements, and these have been the subject of numerous critical studies, particularly in the papers of the Battle Conference and the Haskins Society.

Since the present series is concerned with the peoples of Europe, this book looks at the Normans as a people. It continues their history after the great period of expansion and conquest in the eleventh and early twelfth centuries, up to the nineteenth-century revival of scholarly interest in their history and on to the present day. It is consequently less concerned with the often controversial details of institutional change in the countries where they settled, to which much valuable scholarship has been (and is still being) devoted.

I am indebted to many colleagues with whom I have discussed the Normans at Battle and Cerisy-la-Salle. For help with the illustrations I wish especially to thank Philip Grierson for his photographs of Norman coins, and Lindy Grant and the Librarian of the Conway Library, Courtauld Institute of Fine Art, for help in finding appropriate photographs. The learned staff of Blackwells have been wonderfully patient and long-suffering; in particular my thanks are due to Tessa Harvey and Louise Spencely, and to the picture researchers and copy-editor.

M. C.

Abbreviations

ANS	*Anglo-Norman Studies*
ASC	*Anglo-Saxon Chronicle*
BEC	*Bibliothèque de L'École des Chartes*
BSAN	*Bulletin de la Société des Antiquaires de Normandie*
EHR	*English Historical Review*
GND	*The Gesta Normannorum Ducum* of William of Jumièges
MGH	*Monumenta Germaniae Historica*
SS	*Scriptores*
Migne *PL*	J. P. Migne, *Patrologia Latina*, 221 vols (Paris, 1844–64)
MSAN	Mémoires de la Société des Antiquaires de Normandie
OMT	Oxford Medieval Texts
RS	Rolls Series
TRHS	*Transactions of the Royal Historical Society*
WMGR	William of Malmesbury, *De gestis regum Anglorum*

Part I

People and Duchy

1

The Emergence of a
Norman People

The Norman people were the product, not of blood, but of history. This is true to some extent of all 'peoples'; ethnic purity is largely an illusion. When Strabo surveyed the geography of the world and wrote about the Parthians, Ethiopians, Persians, Libyans, Scythians, Greeks, Romans, and others, he used various terms to describe them,[1] of which *ethne*, loosely translated as 'peoples', came nearest to implying bonds of blood, though this was only one of their characteristics. Of his *History*, which has not survived, he noted that 'only the incidents in the lives of distinguished men are recorded, while deeds that are petty and ignoble are omitted'.[2] This, indeed, points to the way in which history has shaped the peoples of Europe. It is focused on the leading families through many generations; their racial origin gives a name to the group. Yet even these families intermarried with the peoples they conquered. As the Roman Empire crumbled, there were many noble families all over Europe who could provide acceptable brides for the conquering chiefs and the most distinguished of the warriors who dispossessed them. The map of the known world surveyed by Strabo about the time of the Incarnation was already racially mixed. Eight or nine centuries later it was even more dotted with scattered and by no means homogeneous settlements of various peoples.

Even so, the Norman people – the *gens Normannorum* of the chroniclers – were of exceptionally mixed blood. When in the twelfth

[1]   Strabo, I.i.6, 10.
[2]   Strabo, I.i.22, 23.

century the historian Orderic Vitalis attempted to define what was meant by 'Normans', he explained that they were 'men of the North...whose bold roughness had proved as deadly to their softer neighbours as the bitter wind to young flowers'.[3] Their name came from groups of Viking invaders: the men of the sea, who had descended on the shores of north-west Europe from the ninth to the eleventh centuries, first as raiders, then as settlers, preparing themselves to defend the lands they had conquered against the next wave of invaders. Though various groups of Vikings were able to build a short-lived kingdom of York in the north of England, to seize the islands from Orkney and Shetland to Man, to establish settlements in Ireland, and to send bands deep into Francia along the rivers Seine and Loire, it was only in part of the region known as Neustria that they established themselves as a dominant force. Here their identity was recognized by the name 'Normans', and their new homeland was called 'Normandy'. Whereas the Danes, who arrived in eastern England in sufficient numbers for the region where they had settled to be known as the Danelaw, were absorbed into the English kingdom, Normandy became a centre for further expansion, sending Norman knights to conquer England (including the Danelaw) and southern Italy, and to fight for lands in Spain and the Near East. The beginning was slow; the later achievement was lasting. It inspired the Norman leaders to have their exploits recorded by chroniclers, who, from the early eleventh century, left an enduring record of their deeds. Yet at all times the distinguishing feature of the Normans was allegiance to a leader, not ethnic unity. The chroniclers applauded the first Norman counts for successfully welding diverse elements into a single people: a process which, during the periods of expansion, continued in the countries where they settled.[4]

The various Scandinavian invaders themselves were different in custom and organization.[5] The Norwegians tended to work in small groups, and liked to settle in sparsely populated areas, where they intermarried with the indigenous peoples. They were most numerous in the Fatroes, Orkney, Shetland, the Western Isles, and Ireland. They

---

[3] *The Ecclesiastical History of Orderic Vitalis*, ed. M. Chibnall, 6 vols (Oxford, OMT, 1969–80), v. 24–7. See also Radulfus Glaber, *The Five Books of the Histories*, ed. John France (Oxford, OMT, 1989), I. 18, pp. 32–3, 'In their language *Nort* means "the North" and *Mint* "a people"; hence they are called Normans, the "People of the North".'
[4] There were some similarities in the emergence of the 'Franks' as a people; Edward James, *The Franks* (Oxford, 1988), 8–9.
[5] L. Musset, *Les Peuples scandinaves au moyen-âge* (Paris, 1951), esp. 52–64.

rarely departed from the customs of their own country, loosely interpreted. The Danes, on the other hand, worked in large bands, out for a
common profit; they had the cohesion of an army, and readily obeyed
a chief according to the law of the army, which approximated to the
provincial laws of their fatherland. Danish bands provided the bulk of
the settlers in Normandy, where their chiefs were able to maintain a
strict authority. Norwegian elements from Ireland also contributed to
the settlement of the region; but in spite of their dominance the men of
the north were never more than a minority of the population.[6]

The great enigma of Norman history is why the Northmen, who
first settled around the Seine estuary, were able to build a principality ✳
so compact and powerful that it took their name and became a springboard for wider expansion, and even the conquest of an existing
kingdom, before sinking back to the status of a single province
among all the provinces of France. The late eleventh- and twelfth-
century Normans, conscious of the far-flung victories of their compatriots, praised them so eloquently in history and epic song that their
achievements seem at times to be lost in the Norman myth. They
cherished their legends, some of which go beyond the limits of cred-
ibility. But most, even when coloured by imagination, were inspired by
real events. Besides this, for two hundred years the Norman people,
formed by history rather than by race, were as real as the rich and
thriving province of Normandy was to be for the next millennium.

The province that later became Normandy had no clear geographical or ethnic boundaries. It extended along the northern seaboard of
France approximately from the estuary of the Couesnon to that of the
Bresle, taking in the areas drained by the smaller rivers flowing into
the Channel and the lower reaches of the Seine, its principal waterway.
The watershed between these rivers and the tributaries of the Loire
provided only a very rough southern frontier; the eastern and western
boundaries were even more shadowy. Before the Roman conquest the
whole region along the northern sea coast was described as Armorica
(meaning 'the land facing the sea');[7] it was open to influences from
across the Channel, and Strabo noted that some of the tribes settled
along the coast, the Caletes and the Luxovii, were actively engaged in
trade with the British Isles.[8] Julius Caesar referred to regular com-

---

[6] See map 1.
[7] P. Gaillou and M. Jones, *The Bretons* (Oxford, 1991), 7.
[8] Strabo, IV.i.14.
[9] Caesar, *De bello gallico*, v.13, 14.

munications between the Belgae and Kent.[9] The Roman conquest of Britain increased cross-Channel commerce; it also provoked a southward movement of British people escaping from Roman dominance into western Armorica, where they settled among the indigenous peoples and gave their name to Brittany.[10] The later divisions were beginning to take shape, though the eastern seaboard and its hinterland, which were now called Neustria, took in a region extending southwards to the Loire, three times the size of later Normandy.

Roman roads and Roman instruments of government first gave tighter regional administration, with the city of Rouen at its heart. Rouen remained central after the spread of Christianity, and in time its church became metropolitan, though the boundaries of the ecclesiastical province of Rouen never quite coincided with those of the later duchy.

In the city of Rouen there is no church like San Clemente in Rome, where one may plunge down through the layers of history from a medieval church to the foundations of a Roman villa and a pagan shrine. Nevertheless, archaeological discoveries have begun to reveal the early history of the city, and these encapsulate the first stages of the history of the making of Normandy.[11] Foundations of Roman houses show the first settlements in what appears to have been an open town, without fortifications, where a small urban aristocracy enjoyed the Roman creature comforts of heating and baths up to the third century AD. There are signs too of economic activity, chiefly of small artisan workshops; the road system shows that the town was a centre of mostly land-borne trade and the river Seine provided another route to the interior. A little later, evidence of hidden money hoards and fires begins, probably at the time of the first Frankish invasions between AD 253 and 270. The first defensive ramparts were probably constructed shortly after Rouen was made the capital of the Roman province of the Second Lyonnaise. Excavations indicate that large buildings, probably part of military quarters, were superimposed on the sites of the burnt houses; they could have been the installations of the garrison of *Ursarii*, one of the forces of auxiliaries put in charge of the frontier regions of the empire, whose presence in Rouen about the middle of the fourth century is listed in the *Notitia Dignitatum*. There were also new houses, smaller than the last; and traces of

[10] Gaillou and Jones, 128–30.
[11] Michel Maugard, 'Rouen antique', in *Histoire de Rouen*, ed. Michel Mollat (Toulouse, 1979), ch. 2.

church buildings appear for the first time on the site where the later cathedral was to be built.

Rome created an administrative system in which Rouen was at the heart of the Second Lyonnaise. As the Roman Empire crumbled, effective civil government broke down, leaving the Church to take over and preserve provincial administration during the first centuries of the Frankish kingdom. Later traditions named St Mallon as the first bishop of Rouen; but his name is not recorded in any texts before the ninth century. Bishop Avitianus, known to have attended the Council of Arles in 314, is the first authenticated bishop. He must have had a church in Rouen, though the first written evidence of church building comes in the time of St Victricius, a learned man and an active missionary, who visited Italy. From there he brought back relics of SS Gervase and Protais, given to him by St Ambrose of Milan. It was to house these that Victricius built a new basilica *c.* 396, as his treatise *De laude sanctorum* vividly describes. His own sweat had, he claimed, watered the soil as he carried huge stones: would that his blood could have watered it as well![12] Jacques Le Maho has identified the basilica of late fourth-century date as the church of Victricius, and conjectured that it was probably parallel to an earlier basilica of which nothing remains.[13] The two were later joined by an atrium, and were at the heart of the first cathedral complex. As yet there were no burials there; according to the Roman practice these took place in churches outside the city, such as St Godard, which probably housed the relics of St Romanus. Only when the ninth-century Viking invasions led to the abandonment of settlements outside the walls did the first tombs appear in the cathedral precincts.

Active life in the church of Rouen continued under the Merovingian kings. Archaeological remains from the mid-eighth century have been identified as communal buildings, constructed in the time of Archbishop Remigius. It was he who, in the 760s, reformed his cathedral chapter, installed secular canons following the rule of St Chrodegang, and provided them with separate endowment out of the revenues of the archbishop. Excavations have revealed traces of a dormitory, a large room (the *domus dispensatoria*) where alms were distributed, a

---

[12] *De laude sanctorum*, in Migne *PL* 20, cols 443–58; Paul Grosjean, 'Notes', *Analecta Bollandiana*, 63 (1945), 94–9.
[13] J. Le Maho, 'Le groupe épiscopal de Rouen du IVe au Xe siècle', in *Medieval Art, Architecture and Archaeology at Rouen*, ed. Jenny Stratford (British Archaeological Association Conference Transactions, 12 (1993 for 1986)), 20–9, at 20–3.
[14] Ibid., 24–9.

cloister with houses for the canons, and a building that may have been a library.[14] Building works, including the installation of an aqueduct, continued into the ninth century. The Church, which had preserved the framework of Roman government, was clearly wealthy, influential, and a centre of some culture. Monasteries were founded and endowed by a number of noble Franks at Rouen (Saint-Ouen), Fontenelle (later Saint-Wandrille), Jumièges, Fécamp, Montivilliers, and elsewhere. Some of the bishops were holy men who attracted local cults. Others were imposed by Merovingian and later Carolingian rulers who were aware of the wealth and influence of the see. In spite of local disorders, the region remained relatively stable. Even when, under the first Carolingians, the centre of gravity in their kingdom moved eastwards from Neustria to Austrasia, Neustria was not forgotten. Charlemagne came twice to Rouen; Charles the Bald also visited Neustria, though for military and diplomatic reasons he chose to stay in the palace of Pîtres, near Pont-de-l'Arche. The relative peace and prosperity of the region were destroyed when Viking raids began in the ninth century.[15] Their impact is visible in the charred remains of the cathedral complex in the heart of Rouen; the history of their settlement is that of the rise of the duchy of Normandy.

[15]　L. Musset, 'Naissance de la Normandie', in *Histoire de Normandie*, ed. M. de Bouard (Toulouse, 1970), 83–91.

2

The Rise of Normandy

The rise of Normandy was part of the process which brought about
the emergence of the provinces of France.[1] New Germanic invaders
were gradually absorbed. The Saxons made little impact; though there
are references in Gregory of Tours to the 'Saxons of Bayeux' we have
little information about them. The Franks were much more influential. After their conquests under Clovis in the later fifth century, they
gained control of Gaul north of the Loire, with the exception of
Brittany. Once established, they showed themselves willing to work
within existing structures. The new aristocracy, which gradually infiltrated into, but did not entirely replace, the old, was a rural aristocracy of great estates; beneath them much of the indigenous population
remained and continued to till the land. They took over many of the
administrative divisions of the Roman Empire; the ancient *pagus*
frequently became the *comté*, though some *pagi* were divided into
two and one disappeared altogether. Civil administration was reinforced by the main structure of the Gallo-Roman Church, which
survived. Moreover, the Franks in Neustria, unlike those in Austrasia,
were prepared to adopt the Latin language. Law was more personal;
legal custom derived from Salic law developed alongside Roman
customary law. Lucien Musset considered that one of the most durable
legacies of the Merovingian regime was the introduction of a law that
was essentially Germanic and which, under successive forms, first of
Salic law, then of custom, prevailed in Normandy right up to 1789.[2]

---

[1] K. F. Werner, 'Quelques observations au sujet des débuts du "duché" de Normandie', in
Droit privé et institutions régionales: Études historiques offertes à Jean Yver (Paris, 1976),
691–709.
[2] Musset, 'Naissance', 80–1.

The depth of Germanic penetration varied in upper Normandy, where Frankish influence was strongest, and in lower Normandy, more open to influences from Britain. In spite of this, under the Merovingians the Second Lyonnaise was becoming a region with its own characteristics, distinct from Brittany to the west and the former Belgic provinces to the east. The region was prosperous; agriculture flourished, and the network of Roman roads branching out from Rouen made it a centre of trade. The administrative framework of Roman government had been preserved to some extent by the Church, and the monasteries were centres of religion and learning. On the debit side, the military organization was weak, and this left the region open to plunder while its natural resources tempted raiders.

The first notices of Viking raids appeared in chronicles when attacks began along the coast of Flanders during the reign of Charlemagne. At this date the Northmen were seeking plunder and made no attempt to settle. For a time they turned aside to attack England and Ireland. The *Anglo-Saxon Chronicle* recorded their first appearance off the English coast in 789, and from 835, when they ravaged Sheppey, references to attacks by Danes or 'heathen men' occur repeatedly in the *Chronicle*. Before the middle of the ninth century they had returned to raid along the coasts of Gaul. By sailing up the rivers they struck further inland. Their movements were recorded in contemporary Frankish annals; the attempts to drive them back are noted also in the *Capitularia Regum Francorum*.[3] In 841 Rouen and Jumièges were burnt; an expedition in 845 reached Paris. Attacks on Brittany were fought off,[4] but in 851, for the first time, the Vikings wintered along the lower Seine from 13 October to 5 June. Their attacks on monasteries forced the monks of Noirmoutiers (in Brittany) and Saint-Philbert to seek refuge at Cunault in Anjou, carrying with them the relics of their saints; by 875 they had moved further inland to Tournus in Burgundy.

Different war bands attacked up the rivers Seine and Loire. Charles the Bald endeavoured to mobilize forces against them; between 865 and 868 he had fortifications built at Pîtres near Pont-de-l'Arche, in an attempt to prevent raiders sailing up the Seine.[5] On the Loire, where invaders penetrated to Angers, Tours and Orleans, the king sought local allies among the Bretons. Their ambitious leader, Salomon, had

[3] The *'Gesta normannorum ducum'* of *William of Jumièges, Orderic Vitalis, and Robert of Torigni*, ed. E. M. C. van Houts, 2 vols (Oxford, OMT, 1992–5), i. 20.
[4] Gaillou and Jones, 166–7.
[5] F. Lot, 'Le Pont-de-Pîtres', *Le Moyen Age*, 2ᵉ série, 9 (1905), 1–33.

successfully usurped power in 857; in 863 territory was ceded to him, and in 867 he was granted control of the Cotentin, with its revenues, the royal estates, and everything except the bishopric. To these concessions was added the title of 'king'. His status as a provincial governor was short-lived, and Breton power collapsed after his death.[6] Nevertheless it was a precedent for handing over the task of defence to a local power under a Frankish 'king'. It was only a short step to making similar concessions for the same purpose to a Viking leader.

The history of the bands who attacked the coast of Gaul after 790 and in time won control of the lower Seine became entangled in legends. These gathered round the names of war leaders, circulated in England, Normandy and Scandinavia, and were written down in various garbled versions by the earliest historians of the Normans. The exploits of Hasting and Björn Ironside became inextricably entangled.[7] A legendary expedition, which penetrated into the Mediterranean with the purpose of capturing Rome, but was diverted to *Luna* near Pisa, was attributed to Hasting. Björn was sometimes called the son of King Lodbroc, who may have been the same as the Viking hero Ragnar Loðbrók. But however varied the identifications in song and oral history, some events can be connected with entries in more sober chronicles and Frankish annals contemporary with the invasions. These, however, more frequently name the cities besieged or burnt than the leaders of the attacking bands.

The leader who emerged clearly in the early tenth century was Rolf or Rollo.[8] He was probably a Norwegian, the son of Rögnvald, earl of Möre. Shortage of land and numerous kin compelled him, like so many of his well-born compatriots, to seek his fortune abroad. The followers he brought together to attack the coasts of Scotland, Ireland, and finally Neustria, were mostly Danes. Well-disciplined and bound by the law of the army, they were a force to be reckoned with. When, in 911, Rollo led them in an unsuccessful siege of Chartres, they were formidable enough to persuade Charles the Simple that they might be turned into valuable allies, as the Bretons under Salomon had been. At some date, traditionally assigned to 911 and certainly before 918,

---

[6] *GND* i. 20–1.

[7] E. M. C. van Houts, 'Scandinavian influence in Norman literature of the eleventh century', *ANS*, 6 (1984), 107–21; *GND* i. pp. xxxvi–xxxviii, 16–27; F. Amory, 'The Viking Hasting in Franco-Scandinavian legend', in *Saints, Scholars and Heroes: Studies in Medieval Culture in Honour of C. W. Jones* (Minnesota, 1979), 269–86.

[8] *Dudo of St Quentin. History of the Normans*, trans. Eric Christiansen (Woodbridge, 1998), p. xix and n. 29.

Charles substituted diplomacy for force. He met Rollo, probably at Saint-Clair-sur-Epte, and ceded lands round the lower Seine to him and his followers. Rollo was to undertake full responsibility for the defence of the Seine against all attacks; he promised not to invade other Frankish lands, to accept baptism, and to swear fealty to the king. Whatever this oath implied, it was certainly not vassalage as it was later understood in a more feudal society.

The lands ceded to Rollo consisted of the territory of the Roman city (*civitas*) of Rouen, the *pagus* dependent on it, and a few annexed territories.[9] It was roughly bounded by the Bresle, the Epte and the Avre, and was smaller than the ecclesiastical province of Rouen. The Vexin was cut in two. Rollo may from the outset have aimed at far more, but he showed himself to have some diplomatic talents, and moved by slow stages. He recognized that he must work with the king and the indigenous population, and this involved accepting their religion. He was baptized, and took the first steps towards restoring the Church. The archbishop and clergy who had fled during the invasions were recalled to Rouen, and some monks were brought back to the abbey of Saint-Ouen. The statement of Dudo of Saint-Quentin a century later, that he also married the king's daughter Gisela, is unsupported by contemporary evidence;[10] his handfast wife or concubine, Poppa, was the mother of his son William Longsword.

Within some twenty years the authority of the new Scandinavian leaders in Rouen had extended much further. The subject is poorly documented; but, as John Le Patourel wrote, it seems from the scanty evidence 'that war and conquest were quite as important in the territorial formation of Normandy as legitimate royal grant', also that 'this process took longer, was more complex and less tidy in its ultimate outcome, than the customary interpretation of three "grants" of 911, 924 and 933 would imply.'[11] Each territorial gain seems to have been regarded as providing 'a base of operations for future wars'. According to Dudo of Saint-Quentin, followed by William of Jumièges, Rollo designated his son William as his successor five years before he died and persuaded his principal followers to swear to accept him.[12] What-

[9]   Musset, 'Naissance', 101–3.
[10] Dudo, section 169, trans. Christiansen, 49.
[11] J. Le Patourel, *The Norman Empire* (Oxford, 1976), 5.
[12] Dudo, ed. Lair, 180–2, trans. Christiansen, 58–60; *GND* i. 72–3. The succession is discussed by J. Le Patourel, 'The Norman succession, 996–1135', *EHR*, 86 (1971), 225–50; G. Garnett, '"Ducal" succession in early Normandy', in *Law and Government in Medieval England and Normandy: Essays in Honour of Sir James Holt* (Cambridge, 1994), 80–110.

ever the truth of this, after Rollo's death at a date around 930, William had to contend with attacks by Bretons and bands of Northmen (treated as 'rebels' in the later Norman chronicles), who rejected his authority. He found allies among the Franks, who were themselves torn by rivalries and disputed successions. Frankish support meant that he was able to secure approval for his occupation of the Avranchin and the Cotentin, previously granted to the Breton ruler Salomon, but now open to new predators because of divisions between the Bretons themselves.[13] By 933 the Normans of the Seine had a precarious hold on almost all the territories that later made up Normandy. But their Frankish involvement brought new enemies, and in 942 William (Longsword) was treacherously murdered at Picquigny on the Somme by Arnold of Flanders. He had already, possibly following the precedent set by his father, secured an oath from his followers to accept his son Richard as his successor. Unfortunately when he was murdered Richard was only ten years old.[14]

Whatever doubts may have been felt about the religious convictions of Rollo, even after his baptism with the name of Robert, William's whole-hearted devotion to the Christian Church was well attested. He began the restoration of the abbey of Jumièges with monks brought from Saint-Cyprian at Poitiers accompanied by their abbot Martin; according to the account of William of Jumièges, based partly on Dudo, he would have become a monk there had not Abbot Martin dissuaded him by pointing out the difficulties his young son Richard would then face.[15] In the event his murder left young Richard at the mercy of warring parties.

Both King Louis and his most powerful vassal, Hugh the Great, took advantage of Richard's minority, Louis to establish himself at Rouen with Richard a virtual prisoner at Laon, and Hugh to occupy Bayeux. It was five years before Richard, helped by loyal friends, was able to take full command of Rouen and the territories held by his father. His success opened up a new phase in the rise of Normandy.[16] Up to then the Northmen of the Seine must have seemed to contemporaries as no more firmly settled than the other bands who had held temporary sway in the region of the Loire and Brittany, or in the kingdom of York. From that time the consolidation of their authority

---

[13] Gaillou and Jones, 167–8.
[14] *GND* i. 88–95.
[15] *GND* i. 86–9.
[16] Musset, 'Naissance', 110.

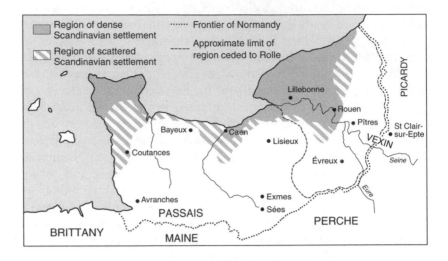

Map 1   *Normandy in the mid-eleventh century*

and the establishment of a duchy that was the most nearly independent of all the provinces of France began. More time was still needed for a people to emerge who might be generally recognized as 'Normans'.

The population was ethnically mixed from the outset. In spite of lurid accounts of devastation caused by the Vikings, the looting of church treasures and the destruction of libraries, the region was never reduced to anything like a desert. There had been only a little Scandinavian settlement before 911, and even after that date mass settlement never took place. Widely distributed, the immigrants never expropriated the indigenous population whom they dominated. In the country they occupied abandoned or thinly populated regions; along the coast their influence on the maritime vocabulary suggests slightly denser settlement.[17] Apart from the first group of Rollo's men, they arrived in different war-bands from various countries. Many settlers in the Cotentin were Norwegian, coming possibly from Ireland. In the 930s a band appears at Bayeux, which seems, from the Anglo-Scandinavian rural vocabulary that it left behind, to have migrated from England.[18] A decade later we hear of an army led by a Dane called Harold, whom some chroniclers wrongly confused with a later king Harold Bluetooth; he helped to maintain order after the murder of

[17]   See map 1.
[18]   Musset, 'Naissance', 101–6.

William Longsword in 942. Language caused no serious problems among the settlers; linguistically the Scandinavian peoples had a similar vernacular, known as 'the Danish tongue',[19] and they accepted the Latin culture of the Church and the Frankish kings. The high proportion of male settlers necessitated intermarriage with the indigenous people.

Machiavelli was much later to claim that the essentials for any principality were good laws and good arms, adding that laws could not be upheld without good arms. For the emerging people of the Normans this was certainly true. Their leaders enforced the 'law of the army', which had held together the war-bands of invaders, and later – in spite of rebellions and attacks from outside – bound together the peoples of the emerging duchy. They took advantage of the rivalries that weakened the divided and declining Frankish empire in the years before the Capetians came to power. By the end of the tenth century the ruling Norman family had survived the minority of William Longsword's young son, Richard, and the attacks made by rulers of provinces bordering their territory. On one occasion, threatened by the Frankish king, they brought in Scandinavian allies to ravage his lands. Once Hugh Capet had won the crown and established the dynasty of the former counts of Paris on the throne of France in 987, external relations were simplified, even though Hugh's authority was at first little more than nominal and ill-defined. The title 'duke' began to be applied to the Norman counts of Rouen some time after 987, possibly shortly before the death of Richard I in 996.[20] Hitherto the official title had been 'count' or 'princeps'; it is even doubtful if Rollo had any title. A careful contemporary, Fulbert of Chartres, addressed Richard II as 'optime princeps', but never used the ducal title.[21] 'Duke' might be used by a rhetorical writer in the sense of 'leader', as when Richer of Reims referred to Richard I as 'dux pyratorum' ('leader of the pirates'); but 'dux' had no administrative significance.

Gradually contemporaries began to think of the Northmen of the Seine as Normans. By the time Richard II succeeded his father in 996 language was catching up with political reality, and royal documents

[19] Frederic Amory, 'The *dönsk tunga* in early medieval Normandy. A note', in *Trends and Linguistics, Studies and Monographs 16, Papers in Honor of Madison S. Beeler*, ed. K. Klar and S. Silver (The Hague, Paris, New York, 1980), 279–89.

[20] Werner, 'Quelques observations', 691–709. The earliest known authentic Norman charter using the title 'duke' is the diploma of Richard II for Fécamp, 1006 (Fauroux, no. 9).

[21] Fulbert of Chartres (*c*.1023) addressed Richard II as 'Venerando Normannorum principi'; 'obtime princeps' occurs in the text of the letter (*The Letters and Poems of Fulbert of Chartres*, ed. Frederick Behrends (Oxford, OMT, 1976), no. 83, p. 150).

gave official sanction to the title 'Duke of the Normans'. In Richard's
reign, from 996 to 1027, a Norman culture began to take shape. To
the external, often fragmentary sources, are added documents issued
from the ducal writing office, the annals of Norman religious houses,
and histories of the dukes. When the Normans took up the writing of
their history in the eleventh century they transformed it, scooping up
all the legends and making the duchy an instant creation of the year
911. They built, more authentically (but not without imaginative
improvement) on these foundations. That is their myth, but they
themselves were real enough as a people – always allowing for the
fact that they were a people formed out of diverse races.

The written history of the dukes of Normandy dates from about the
time that the ducal title was recognized. Dudo of Saint-Quentin
claimed that Richard I had persuaded him to 'describe the customs
and deeds of the Norman lords' two years before his death.[22] Dudo
wrote it in the reign of Richard II (996–1026), with encouragement
from the duke himself and much information from the duke's half-
brother, Raoul, count of Ivry. Oral no less than written tradition
determined the form it was to take. At the heart of tenth-century
secular history was family tradition. The author of the Icelandic
Book of Settlements (*Landnámabók*), writing in the early twelfth
century, expressed a widely felt sentiment when he defended writing
the history of the settlements:

> For those men who want to know old lore or to reckon genealogies, it is
> better to begin at the beginning rather than to jump right into the
> middle. And of course all wise peoples want to know about the begin-
> nings of their own settlement and of their own families.[23]

When the family commemorated was that of a leader, the record might
become the history of a people, and the genealogy might be traced
back to a god or – in a Christian society – to a Trojan leader.

Dudo himself came from Picardy, and was educated in the schools
there at a time when no adequate schools existed in Normandy. A
canon, later dean, of Saint-Quentin, he was brought to Normandy by
Richard I in about 994, and stayed on as a ducal chaplain at the court
of Richard II. Some charters were drafted by him as 'Dudo, chancellor' – a title which, at that date, probably meant simply that he was at

---

[22]   Dudo, sections 119–20; trans. Christiansen, 6.
[23]   Cited Jesse L. Byock, *Medieval Iceland. Society, Sagas and Power* (Enfield Lock,
1993), 14.

the head of the duke's writing office.[24] At Saint-Quentin he had learned to write in a high-flown literary style, and had read widely in literary sources. He knew, amongst other works, the *Etymologies* of Isidore of Seville, Paul the Deacon's *History of the Lombards*, the work of Jordanès on the Goths, and a chronicle of Frankish history. To the literary tradition of the histories of peoples, he added Scandinavian legends of the deeds of earlier Vikings.[25] The achievements that he admired in the first Norman leaders were those of converting the pagan Vikings to Christianity, and bringing together peoples of many different races to live in harmony under their duke. His own achievement was similar: to bring together the Frankish and Scandinavian traditions in a history of the Normans as eclectic in its sources as were the peoples themselves. Although he rewrote events to establish a spurious antiquity for the duchy and the ducal authority, his work does not deserve the wholesale condemnation it has sometimes received. It was the embodiment of Norman culture and aspirations in the first decade of the eleventh century; and it initiated a long tradition of historical writing that accompanied the Normans wherever they established principalities. Hearing the exploits of their ancestors and the Norman people was one of the recreations of Norman rulers during the long winter evenings. As Geoffrey of Malaterra wrote (citing Sallust), to explain why Count Roger of Sicily liked to be entertained by hearing about the deeds of the Normans, 'the desire for fame lifts men above the level of brute beasts, and so justifies the recording of great deeds.'[26]

As the first history of the Norman people, Dudo's work was a response to the need felt by all invaders of the Roman Empire to be accepted as an integral part of the imperial world. This involved first adopting the Latin language and the Christian faith, and second, claiming an ancestry equal in distinction to that of the Romans.[27] Since the most enduring Roman legends traced the foundation of the imperial city to the Trojan Aeneas, and the Christian religion excluded

[24] M. Fauroux, 'Deux autographes de Dudo de Saint-Quentin', *BEC*, 111 (1953), 229–34. Original in Archives de la Seine-Maritime, 14H, 915A.
[25] The influences on his work have been discussed most recently by Christiansen, *Dudo*, pp. xvii–xxix. For different views see E. Searle, 'Fact and pattern in heroic history: Dudo of St Quentin', *Viator*, 15 (1984), 75–84; R. H. C. Davis, *The Normans and their Myth* (London, 1976).
[26] Malaterra, p. 4.
[27] R. W. Southern, 'Aspects of the European tradition of historical writing. 1. The classical tradition from Einhard to Geoffrey of Monmouth', *TRHS*, 5th series, 20 (1970), 173–96, at 188–95.

any claim to descent from a god, the newer peoples, whether Franks, Saxons, Normans or their like, claimed descent from different groups of Trojans fleeing from the sack of Troy. Widukind, writing about 970, recorded an oral tradition that the Saxons were descended from the remnants of Alexander the Great's army, who in turn were descended from followers of Priam settled in Macedonia.[28] Whether or not Dudo knew the work of Widukind, he was familiar with the stories of Trojan origins widespread in literary and popular traditions.

His history began with a general consideration of the ancestry of the Northmen and the region from which they had come; it was made up of a blend of Latin writings such as that of Jordanès, Scandinavian legend, and fanciful etymology derived ultimately from Isidore of Seville. The Normans, he claimed, came from Denmark, or Dacia, a land inhabited by a tribe of Goths called Dani, who were descended from the Trojan Antenor, king of Dacia. They were led in their attacks on the Frankish kingdom by the Viking Hasting; the reason for the mass exodus was over-population, which Dudo attributed to polygamy. In his account of the deeds of Hasting and his attacks on Neustria, Dudo relied almost entirely on Scandinavian legends, which were cherished in eleventh-century Rouen, but once he turned to Rollo in his second book the blend of sources becomes more evident. His chapters on Hasting had established the origin of the Norman people (as he saw it) and their warlike characteristics. Rollo's life was to show the influence of Christianity and Latin culture. Dudo attributed a vision to Rollo, foretelling how he would be baptized and would bring together peoples of many races under his rule. He described Rollo's voyage to France in obedience to his vision; when evil spirits attempted to prevent his impending baptism by raising a violent storm, Rollo (anticipating his conversion) prayed to God to check the waves, and the seas became calm[29] – an episode surely borrowed from the lives of Christian saints. When, finally, Rollo came to terms with King Charles the Simple and was granted the future Normandy, he immediately accepted baptism and took the name of Robert. While Dudo exaggerated both the extent of the territories ceded to Rollo and the speed of his conversion from paganism, he perceived the importance of the Church in ensuring the permanence of the Viking settlement. The concessions granted to Rollo, similar in the main to those previously granted to the Bretons in the

[28] *MGH SS in usum scholarum*, ed. P. Hirsch, 20–1.
[29] Dudo, sections 146–9, trans. Christiansen, 29–33; *GND* i. 47–8.

Cotentin, included in addition, as later history was to show, control of the bishoprics.[30] This enabled the later dukes to win favour with popes and churchmen, at least during the early stages of the eleventh-century church reform. It provided them both with loyal practical support from bishops and abbots, who were temporal no less than spiritual lords, and with warm praise in the chronicles of learned monks. Dudo likewise anticipated the extent of the territories they were to rule, and the date of the title 'duke of Normandy'. In this way he put the seal of imagined antiquity on the status and power that Rollo and his descendants had won with difficulty during nearly a hundred years. Yet if he did violence to chronology, he was true to both the ambition and the potential of Rollo's Northmen, who laid the foundations of Normandy.

Dudo wrote to please his patrons, but he was not alone in his admiration of Normandy under Duke Richard II. Raoul Glaber, a Cluniac monk writing a little later in Burgundy, was equally laudatory. He wrote that after Rollo and his Normans were converted to Christianity an outstanding line of dukes arose. He declared that,

> Rouen was the metropolitan city of this ducal principality. The dukes surpassed all men in military might, in their desire for a general peace, and in their liberality. The whole province subject to their sway lived as one stock or one family united in harmony and unbroken faith. Amongst these people anyone who, in any transaction, took more than was just from another, or falsely described any merchandise, was regarded as no better than a thief or a robber. The needy, the poor, and all pilgrims were treated with the constant care which fathers show to sons. They made generous gifts to the churches of almost the whole world.[31]

Perhaps Raoul Glaber's admiration was coloured by his respect for St William of Dijon, the Cluniac abbot who was to play an important part in reviving monastic life in Normandy. But it shows that by the second quarter of the eleventh century the Norman dukes were beginning to attract attention because of the relative peace and order they had established in Normandy. In spite of intermittent rebellions and outbreaks of disorder, the Normans were laying the foundations that enabled them to use the duchy as a springboard for conquests across

---

[30] Musset, 'Naissance', 97–9.
[31] Glaber, I.20, pp. 36–7.

Europe, and the establishment of Norman dynasties in kingdoms as far apart as England and Sicily.

When Dudo of Saint Quentin first gave shape to the myth of the Norman origins, the duchy of Normandy was still being formed. The Normans had a roughly defined living space; they still needed to stabilize their frontiers and build up an administration. Whatever might have been included in the three 'grants' of 911, 924 and 933, the actual territory controlled by the Normans was gradually determined through the balance of military forces; it never corresponded entirely with the earlier Carolingian *pagi*. In the east, where resistance was encountered from the Capetian kings and the count of Flanders, the frontier settled in time on the line of the river Avre, cutting the Vexin in half. In the west repeated attempts to establish settlements in the region of Dol were frustrated by Breton claims, and time was needed to reduce the influence of the Bretons in the Bessin and the Cotentin, where they had held territory during the strong rule of Salomon. The river Couesnon provided a rough, but contended, boundary. The southern frontier was particularly unstable; it was essentially a marcher region, where some non-Norman families, notably the Bellême, held lands contended by the Norman counts. The Norman diocese of Sées extended into the comté of Mortagne and the lordship of Bellême, 'which were only attached to Normandy as possessions of families who also held land in the duchy'.[32] The most determined efforts at expansion in the early eleventh century came in this region. Much was achieved during the long reign of Duke Richard II (996–1026). A friend and ally of the Capetian king, Robert the Pious, he went further than his predecessors in building on Frankish institutions and adopting Frankish customs, without abandoning the Scandinavian inheritance.[33]

Kinship was important in building up Norman power and, as Eleanor Searle has pointed out, it was predatory kinship.[34] Although the dukes had accepted, with Christianity, the principle of monogamy, Danish custom was still vigorous enough for their bastard sons to enjoy almost full acceptance. Their legitimate marriages helped them to form alliances and strengthened their frontiers; the children of all their unions held most of the positions of dignity and power, including those in the Church. From the beginning of his reign Richard II was

---

[32] Le Patourel, *NE*, 8–13.
[33] Musset, 'Naissance', 111–14.
[34] E. Searle, *Predatory Kinship and the Creation of Norman Power, 840–1066* (Berkeley, 1988).

Table 1 The dukes of Normandy (simplified)

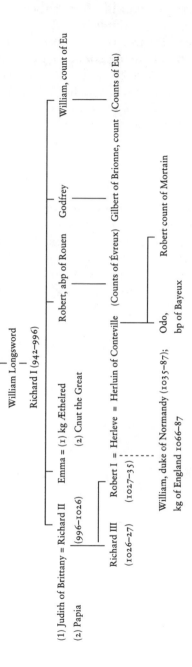

abp = archbishop
bp = bishop
kg = king

helped by his uncle, Raoul of Ivry, the half-brother of Richard I; and from 1010 he used his ducal status to nominate other kinsfolk as counts under himself. His brother Mauger became count of Corbeil; and of his half-brothers, William was made count of Eu, and Godfrey's son, Gilbert of Brionne, was in time given the title of count. His brother Robert, archbishop of Rouen, fathered Richard, later count of Évreux. Two of the sons of Raoul of Ivry became bishops: Hugh of Bayeux and John of Avranches; his daughter Emma married Osbern the steward, a nephew of the duchess Gunnor and later the devoted guardian of the young Duke William.[35]

Marriages helped to stabilize relations with neighbouring rulers. Conflicts with Brittany were checked for a time by a double marriage. Geoffrey, duke of Brittany (992–1028), the son of Conan I, married Duke Richard II's sister Hawise, and Richard himself married Geoffrey's sister Judith. After Geoffrey's death on a pilgrimage to Rome, Duke Richard became the guardian of his two sons, Alan and Eudes.[36] So began a period in which the dukes of Normandy claimed with varying success some type of lordship over Brittany; and in spite of renewed hostilities in the time of Robert I (1027–35), the Norman dukes succeeded in tightening their hold on the territory up to the river Couesnon, and firmly establishing their influence in Mont-Saint-Michel. Another marriage was even more momentous in its consequences. Duke Richard II's sister, Emma, became the wife of King Æthelred of England, and established a bond that was later to provide Duke William with a claim to succeed to the throne of England by hereditary right.

The death of Richard II in 1026 was followed by a short period of greater instability. His son, Richard III, lived for little more than a year, and then, in the words of William of Jumièges, 'as some people say, he died of poison, leaving his brother as his heir to the duchy'.[37] In the next century William of Malmesbury improved the story by adding, 'There is a widespread rumour that he was poisoned with the connivance of his brother Robert.'[38] Whatever the truth of this, Robert was the nearest blood relative with a good claim to succeed, since Richard's only son, Nicholas, a monk at Saint-Ouen, Rouen, was almost certainly illegitimate. Robert had to face some rebellions in the early years of his reign, especially from William of Bellême on the

[35] See table 1.
[36] Gaillou and Jones, 188–91.
[37] *GND* ii. 46–7.
[38] *WMGR* 211. See the comments of D. C. Douglas on poisoning in eleventh-century Normandy (Douglas, *WC*, App. F, 408–15).

southern frontier; but much of his military strength was used to help both Baldwin, count of Flanders, and Henry, king of the French, in times of difficulty. His seizure of many monastic estates was probably due to a need to pay for his wars; perhaps because he later restored much of the value of lands taken he was remembered by William of Jumièges as a devout and faithful Christian.[39]

The most serious troubles came when he died in 1035, leaving as his heir his illegitimate son William, who was barely eight years old. He had taken the precaution of requiring his vassals to accept the boy, William, as his heir; it is possible too that he obtained the consent of King Henry I of France. In spite of this, for Duke Robert to have gone on a dangerous pilgrimage in such circumstances may seem reckless.[40] Although he may have been stirred by the movement to visit Jerusalem at the time of the 1033 millennium of Christ's death, his action gives some credence to the suspicions that he may not have been entirely guiltless in his brother's death. It was only thanks to the loyalty of a close circle of vassals who protected the young duke that William survived to take over the government of the duchy, and rule for the half century when the Normans began the remarkable expansion that made them indeed one of the 'peoples of Europe'.

'I was brought up in arms from childhood' are words attributed to Duke William on his death-bed by Orderic Vitalis.[41] During the years of his minority his succession, and even his life, were constantly at risk. He was saved by the loyalty of his kindred and his father's friends, notably Robert, archbishop of Rouen (who was also count of Évreux), Count Gilbert of Brionne, Osbern, the steward, and his tutor (*nutricius*), Turchetil or Thurkill of Neufmarché. Among humbler supporters were members of the family of his mother Herleve, including her brothers and Herluin, *vicomte* of Conteville, the husband given her by Duke Robert.[42] After Archbishop Robert's death in 1037, his successor in the see was William's kinsman, Mauger, whose loyalty to a bastard duke was less dependable once other legitimate members of the family advanced claims later in the reign. Thurkill, Osbern and Count Gilbert were all murdered in an ambush in 1041, and further rebellions were instigated by William's cousin Guy of Burgundy in 1047, and Archbishop Mauger's brother, William count of Arques, a few years later. From 1148, however, when

[39] *GND* ii. 54–5, 100–1.
[40] Glaber, IV.20, 21, pp. 202–5.
[41] Orderic, iv. 80–1.
[42] For her family see Douglas, *WC*, App. A, 379–82.

Guy of Burgundy and his supporters were defeated at Val-ès-Dunes, the initiative was in Duke William's hands and he was able to consolidate his power and strengthen his frontiers. In common with his ancestor, Duke Richard I, and his own descendants Henry I and Henry II, he showed that a difficult boyhood could prove the best possible apprenticeship for strong and successful rule later. And, as Orderic Vitalis was never tired of asserting, 'If the Normans are disciplined under a just and firm rule they are men of great valour, who press invincibly to the fore in arduous undertakings, and prove their strength by fighting resolutely to overcome all enemies.'[43]

The chronicles which describe the lives of the dukes of Normandy are dominated by two themes: their success in war, and their benefactions to the Church. A subsidiary theme is their firm enforcement of just laws; however ruthless, they are never described as tyrants in the Norman chronicles. Warfare has been aptly called the national industry of the Normans, and it was as fighting men that they were most praised by their fellow-countrymen and remembered, with admiration as well as hatred, by their enemies.

x   The success of the Normans in the field is a remarkable tribute to their adaptability. The Scandinavian settlers had been a seafaring people: on land horses were useful to them for lightning raids, but they fought on foot. By the time the duchy of Normandy was established they had mastered the art of mounted combat, and were becoming known as valuable allies. This was achieved by temperament and training; and training began young. The comment of Geoffrey of Malaterra at the end of the eleventh century, that 'Arms and horses and the exercises of hunting and hawking are the delight of the Normans', would have been equally true much earlier.[44] Any young man whose family could find the means to equip him with a horse could hope to train as a mounted warrior (plate 1). The sons of ducal kinsmen and vassals might hope to be placed as young boys in lordly households, where their days would be spent training in the management of horses and weapons, including javelins, lances, and bows and arrows. Glimpses of family life in the pages of Orderic Vitalis show that even the young men who did not reside in the household of their lord trained together in groups: it is almost a foretaste of the contrast between boarding and day school in the twentieth century. A group of brothers from the Giroie family, with their younger dependants, can

[43]   Orderic, iii. 98–9; iv. 82–3; v. 24–7.
[44]   Malaterra, I. iii, p. 8.

Plate 1   *South transept of the church of St Georges-de-Boscherville, showing eleventh-century carving of knights (from J. S. Cotman,* Architectural Antiquities of Normandy *(1822), plate VIII). By permission of the Syndics of Cambridge University Library.*

be seen practising physical sports on their way back from a gathering of some kind in a nearby castle. Sports were almost as dangerous as war. Arnold, the eldest son, had a fall against a sharp stone during a friendly wrestling match with another young man at Montreuil, and sustained fatal injuries. Hugh, the sixth son, died in the flower of youth; on the way back from the castle of Sainte-Scolasse he was practising hurling javelins with a number of others, when a badly thrown weapon injured him fatally. Training came sometimes not in friendly practice, but in the harsher school of warfare when civil order broke down. Fulk, another of the Giroie brothers, was evidently taken into the household of Count Gilbert of Brionne during the disorders of Duke William the Bastard's minority; he was riding in the count's bodyguard when his lord was ambushed and was murdered with him.[45]

Survival depended on the skilled use of arms; given the basic equipment, ability might be more important than birth. Although chroniclers liked to mention high birth or noble descent whenever possible, there was no class barrier to a military career. It was scarcely open to peasants, who had neither the equipment nor the training; but even the lord of a modest estate might provide a horse and secure an opening for an active, able-bodied son. All young men of this type mastered the use of the bow and arrow when hunting; for some, it seems plain, archery became the main activity. Normally archers rode to battle and dismounted to shoot. We know all too little about the status and means of selection of the mounted men-at-arms, who formed a very necessary part of Norman armies. The wealthier and more highly born would train in small groups of variable size, often about ten, under a leader (the *magister militum*); they could fight on horseback, charging with the couched lance, hurling javelins, or cutting down their assailants with the sword. If tactics required a part of the army to dismount and fight on foot they were prepared to do so. Much has been made of the formidable impact of a charge with couched lance, which could break through an enemy line; but this was only one element in eleventh-century warfare. Versatility, and the ability to control horses in disciplined manoeuvres, were the qualities that made possible the Norman achievement. These were acquired by lifelong training.

The horse, as Anselm wrote when he compared the equipment of temporal and spiritual knights, was the best friend of the knight: with it he rode to battle, charged the enemy, and, if need arose, escaped from an unsuccessful engagement.[46] Horse-breeding was an essential part of Norman preparations for success in war. By the middle of the eleventh century the superior quality of the Arab and Berber steeds,

---

[45] Orderic, ii. 24–5; *GND* ii. 94–5; see also Malaterra, I. iv, p. 9.

[46] *Memorials of Saint Anselm*, ed. R. W. Southern and F. S. Schmitt, *Auctores Britannici Medii Aevi*, I (London, 1969), 97–102.

mostly acquired from Spain, was recognized. The horse which Duke William rode at the battle of Hastings was said to have been brought from Spain. Normandy itself, however, provided the agricultural resources necessary to support important horse studs, once the best strains had been imported. Several of the greater Norman abbeys, founded in forest regions, were actively involved in horse-breeding.[47] Armour, too, could be provided locally. Deposits of iron in the Norman forests had been worked since Roman times, and charcoal burning to feed the furnaces flourished. Some of the earliest evidence of associations of iron workers comes from Normandy; the valley of the Risle must have rung with the sounds of metal working, and hauberk makers were honoured and rewarded.[48]

If training and equipment were essential to the successful warrior, a safe base in a castle was equally important. Castles, indeed, were the most visible sign of Norman settlement; they were often regarded as a symbol of Norman conquest. They were equally important as residences, and as centres for both defence and attack. A duke's power depended to a great extent on how far he could control the castles in his duchy. One significant passage in which the chronicler William of Jumièges described the disorders of Duke William's minority, records that 'many Normans threw up earthworks in various places and built and fortified strongholds for their own purposes. Once they had established themselves securely in their fortifications, they began to hatch plots and rebellions, and raging fires were lit all over the country.'[49] This description suggests castles of the motte and bailey type – a mound of earth surrounded by a palisade, topped by a wooden structure. Stone castles were still rare in early eleventh-century Normandy (see plate 2). Not surprisingly, once Duke William had successfully asserted his power he insisted on his right to license the building of all substantial castles, and to put his own nominees in charge of any castles, particularly those of the frontier zone, which he did not himself control directly.[50]

[47] In general see R. H. C. Davis, *The Medieval Warhorse: Origin, Development and Redevelopment* (London, 1989); Matthew Bennett, 'The medieval warhorse reconsidered', in *Medieval Knighthood*, 5, ed. Stephen Church and Ruth Harvey (Woodbridge, 1995), 19–40; M. Chibnall, 'Aspects of knighthood: The knight and his horse', in *Chivalry, Knighthood and War in the Middle Ages*, Sewanee Medieval Studies 9, ed. Susan J. Ridyard (Sewanee, 1999), 5–26.
[48] M. Arnoux, *Mineurs, Férons et Maîtres de Forges* (Paris, 1993), 33–6, 47–8, 97–105; Chibnall, *The World of Orderic Vitalis* (Oxford, 1984, repr. Woodbridge, 1996), 68–70.
[49] *GND* ii. 92.
[50] Jean Yver, 'Les châteaux forts en Normandie jusqu 'au milieu du XIIᵉ siècle', *BSAN*, 53 (1957 for 1955–6), 28–115, 604–9.

Plate 2   *The castle of Falaise. By courtesy of Ancient Art and Architecture.*

Almost before the rebellions of his minority had died down, he was actively engaged in strengthening his frontiers, aggressively repelling hostile neighbours, and looking for allies to widen his influence. He needed too to build up his own fighting forces. Whenever possible, he tried to reconcile past rebels, enlarge his household troops, and secure new vassals. He was praised for choosing exile as a preferred punishment for recalcitrant opponents; at first this led to a drift to south Italy or Spain, where trained knights were in demand, until experience taught him that it was better to find some way of retaining such men in his own service. The resolutely hostile were most likely to end their days in prison.

Quite apart from the need for a strong army to defend the frontiers, the Norman way of life required territorial expansion, both to keep the knights in training for war, and to provide new patrimonies for younger sons. If the duke could not hold out hope of substantial rewards, some of the best young knights would be tempted away to permanent service, either with the warring factions in southern Italy or even in the armies of the emperor at Constantinople.

Aristocratic and ducal wealth, as seen by Norman chroniclers, was measured in lands and friends – both vassals and allies. Vassals were bound to their lords by oaths of fealty; they owed counsel and service according to the customs prevailing at the time. If they failed in their duty any land they had received from their lord might be confiscated. Gilbert Crispin's account of the life of Herluin, founder of the Abbey of Bec, describes the relationship which might exist between a well-born vassal and his lord.[51] Herluin had been brought up and trained as a knight in the household of Count Gilbert of Brionne. He had family property and some twenty vassals of his own, and had played a full part in the life of Count Gilbert's court until he refused to act as the count's emissary to Duke Robert of Normandy in a mission he thought unjust. As a result the lands that Herluin held as Gilbert's vassal were forfeited. He still had some property of his own, which he used to establish a small religious community. Custom was flexible and variable; a lord in his court could decide whether it had been infringed and what the penalty would be. There were accepted customs, which guided the behaviour of lords and vassals; they were sufficiently related to the lands held as *feods* or fees by vassals to be described as feudal.

The duke of Normandy enjoyed, in addition to these feudal customs, the ducal rights and revenues belonging to his office. The potential strength of the dukedom was considerable, if the resources were wisely used. Much of Duke William's success depended on his skill in governing men, commanding their allegiance, leading them in battle, and judging them fairly. There were limits to his power that, even though unwritten, could not be overstepped with impunity. His success in defeating opponents and finding allies to press his claims outside the duchy is a measure of his achievement. By any standard, it was remarkable.

William's campaigns involved a prolonged struggle with the counts of Anjou for control of Maine, and with the greatest family whose lands lay across the southern frontier, the Bellême.[52] The struggle was complicated when the king of France realized that Normandy, once regarded as a dependable vassal state, was becoming a dangerous rival for dominance in northern France. Sieges played an important part in the duke's compaigns (see plate 3): strong frontier castles in the hands of rivals were a threat to Normandy, and William's first task was to gain control of the key fortresses of Alencon, within the Norman

---

[51] C. Harper-Bill, 'Herluin, abbot of Bec and his biographer', in *Studies in Church History*, 15, ed. Derek Baker (Oxford, 1978), 15–25.
[52] William of Poitiers, I. 16–40; David Bates, *Normandy before 1066* (London and New York, 1982), ch. 2; Douglas, *WC*, ch. 3; Gillingham, 'William the Bastard at war'.

Plate 3 *Soldiers attack a walled city; from the Bury Bible illuminated by Master Hugo, twelfth century (Corpus Christi College, Cambridge, MS 2, fo. 245b). By courtesy of the Master and Fellows of Corpus Christi College, Cambridge.*

frontiers but held by William of Bellême, and Domfront, in the Passais, which had never previously come into Norman hands. His investment of castles always included throwing up siege-castles, in which a small besieging force could cut off enemy supplies and prevent the garrison from breaking out, whilst the main ducal forces were employed elsewhere. This tactic, together with his speed of movement, sometimes gave the impression that he was in two places at the same time. Once Alençon had fallen and the inhabitants had been brutally terrorized into submission, Domfront was not long in giving way. This was the one victory which, through extending ducal control in the Passais, actually brought a permanent enlargement of Norman territory in the eleventh century. The frontier was fortified, and a strong base for further campaigns in Maine and Anjou was established. When the duke's loyal vassal, Roger of Montgomery, vicomte of the Hiémois, was married to the Bellême heiress, Mabel, a substantial part of the Bellême inheritance was brought more firmly into allegiance to Normandy. Duke William was able to withstand even a major invasion backed by the French king, Henry I. A Norman victory in one of the rare pitched battles of the period, fought at Mortemer in 1054, marked something of a turning-point in the establishment of Norman power.

William's position was further secured by the capture of Guy I, count of Ponthieu, in the battle of Mortemer, for Guy was forced to swear an oath of allegiance to secure his release, and this enabled William to gain the use of valuable harbours, including Saint-Valery, on the Channel coast. Even before this time, Duke William's reputation was sufficiently firmly established to make him a valuable ally. Count Baldwin of Flanders was prepared to give him his daughter Matilda; the marriage was certainly projected as early as 1049, when Pope Leo IX raised objections on obscure grounds of consanguinity in the Council of Reims. Whatever the difficulties, they were quickly overcome and the marriage took place not later than 1051. It gave William the powerful count of Flanders as an ally, and a wife who proved herself capable of sharing some of the burdens of government when her husband was absent on campaigns.

A disputed succession in Maine enabled him to intervene aggressively in the county, and to secure an alliance with the claimant by the betrothal of his eldest son, Robert, to Margaret of Maine when both were still children. Even though Margaret (whose right did not go uncontested) died before the marriage could take place, William chose to consider that the betrothal justified him in claiming Maine on behalf of young Robert. His success was never more than partial; but for a time he had a firm foothold in the politics, ecclesiastical no less than secular, of Maine.

Campaigns in Maine were followed by campaigns on the Breton borders.[53] Internal conflicts in Brittany had undermined the peace established by Duke Richard II; and in 1064 William the Conqueror gave support to a rebel, Rivallon of Combour, against the Breton duke

---

[53] Gaillou and Jones, 190–2.

Conan II, and attracted a number of Breton lords into his service. The
Bretons remained more divided than ever after Conan's death in 1066,
whereas William was secure in Normandy. Any potential dangers
from France had been removed when King Henry died in 1060,
leaving his young son, Philip I, in the guardianship of Count Baldwin
of Flanders. The formidable count of Anjou, Fulk Martel, died in the
same year. Duke William was in an exceptionally strong position, with
a seasoned and well-trained army of household troops and loyal, land-
hungry vassals, when a succession crisis in England began to tempt
him to undertake the greatest enterprise of all.

The strength of his position in Normandy was due not simply to
military exploits. Like the earlier Norman dukes, he had carried on the
work of bringing together the various racial and cultural elements in
his duchy to form a single people. In this work of acculturation the
Church from the first played an important part.

From the time that Rollo accepted baptism, the Norman leaders had
recognized the importance of working with the Church. Initially this
made them more acceptable to the indigenous population they had
conquered; but it was much more than this. Lay literacy seemed on the
point of dying out in north-west Europe; Latin remained the language
of culture, and Latin teaching was becoming the monopoly of clerics.
So clerics provided both the men who wrote letters and charters in the

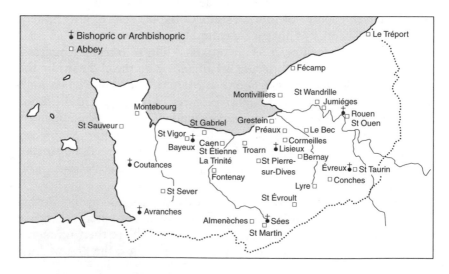

Map 2   *Ecclesiastical Normandy in 1066*

ducal household, and the chroniclers who, from Dudo of Saint-Quentin onwards, recorded the achievements of the Norman leaders and the Norman people. Clerics ordained to the priesthood provided the liturgies of daily life and the solemn ceremonials of baptism into the church militant at birth and departure from it at death. Marriage, though normally a solemn ceremony for the higher aristocracy, could be legal without a church blessing. In addition, bishops and abbots no less than counts were great territorial lords, with wealthy estates and military households. As long as clerical celibacy was not enforced, many bishops expected to be succeeded by a son. The ducal family had a firm grip on many of the bishoprics in the early years of Duke William's reign. Robert, archbishop of Rouen and count of Évreux, a son of Count Richard I, helped to safeguard the succession for Duke William in the first perilous years of his minority; he was succeeded by his nephew Mauger. Duke William gave Bayeux to his half-brother, Odo of Conteville, in 1049. The lineage of Geoffrey, bishop of Coutances, is uncertain, but he may have been distantly related to the duke.

Geoffrey and Odo were outstanding among the episcopal lords who supported the duke both spiritually and temporally.[54] Both found the means to rebuild their cathedrals – Geoffrey by visiting friends in southern Italy and bringing back treasures plundered from Greek churches by the earliest Norman settlers (plate 4). Both encouraged education: Odo by sending clerks destined to be future bishops to study in the famous schools (such as that of Laon) outside Normandy; Geoffrey by establishing a more modest school in his own cathedral to educate the parochial clergy of his diocese. Both served in the ducal court and presided over judicial enquiries before and after the conquest of England. Both brought knights to the ducal armies, and were sometimes involved in campaigns, possibly in the capacity of much later staff officers, but sometimes on the field of battle. Most of their contemporaries saw nothing wrong in this. Orderic Vitalis wrote that Geoffrey was more skilled in teaching knights in hauberks to fight than clerks in vestments to sing psalms, but never accused him of neglecting his duty as a bishop.[55] As John Le Patourel wrote of Geoffrey, 'He was, indeed, a very good specimen of a type of bishop ... whose qualities were of special value in the time of William

---

[54] David Bates, 'The character and career of Odo, bishop of Bayeux', *Speculum*, 50 (1975), 1–20; John Le Patourel, 'Geoffrey of Montbray, bishop of Coutances', *EHR*, 59 (1944), 129–61.
[55] Orderic, iv. 278.

Plate 4   *Capital from Bishop Odo's cathedral of Bayeux, now in the crypt (Conway Library 877/23, 25a). By courtesy of the Conway Library, Courtauld Institute of Art.*

the Conqueror', with the capacity to organize and administer, adding, 'These qualities were needed quite as much in the church as in the secular government, and if Normandy had failed to produce a goodly company of such men in both spheres, William's conquest would have melted away like Cnut's fifty years before.'[56]

Changes in the Church began to spread through western Europe in the eleventh century; but the early reforms enhanced rather than threatened ducal policy. Monasteries played an important part. Duke Richard II began to introduce change by inviting William of Volpiano, abbot of Saint-Benigne at Dijon, to restore monastic life in the community of secular clerks that his father had founded at Fécamp. St William brought with him Cluniac monks and the type of monastic life that he had experienced at Cluny, but the houses he founded, like Saint-Benigne itself, were always independent, never subject to Cluny. The monks of Fécamp, Bernay and other houses

[56] Le Patourel, 'Geoffrey', 157.

that came under his control were disciplined and literate; their monastic schools accepted pupils who were not necessarily destined for monastic life; their liturgy was solemn and dignified, and attention was given to music and good singing. But the spiritual side of monastic life was balanced by the economic; St William insisted that monasteries must have adequate endowments. He also refused to tolerate the giving of money for spiritual offices, which was condemned as simony. His life shows his readiness to work together in friendship with lay powers for their mutual benefit, but not to be dominated by them.[57] In this the dukes of Normandy were willing collaborators. Duke William the Conqueror stated characteristically in one charter granting property to the abbey of Saint-Florent by Saumur, that he had granted it freely, retaining no secular claim, and adding, 'Though we are Normans, we know well that it should be so, and this, God willing, we will do.'[58]

Both Robert and his son William helped to restore the economic fortunes of monasteries such as Jumièges and Fécamp, which had been plundered and reduced almost to ruins in the ninth and tenth centuries. Anxious not to diminish the ducal demesnes more than necessary, they made restitution partly by granting economic privileges, market profits, and the share of tithes that patrons claimed to control. Their gifts, however, included some grants of former church estates that had been secularized. William in particular was praised for founding monasteries and encouraging his vassals to do likewise. Orderic Vitalis stated that on his death-bed William claimed to have enriched the nine abbeys of monks and six of nuns founded in Normandy by his ancestors; also, that when he was duke eighteen other abbeys, including one of nuns, had been established. These included the two abbeys in Caen that he and his wife founded (see plate 5).[59] He kept a decisive voice in the appointment of abbots, and even occasionally forced his own candidate on the monks in what were nominally free elections. He needed to be sure that, in any time of disturbance in the duchy, the wealthy abbeys (particularly those in the frontier region) were not in the hands of enemies.

Moreover the Church was firmly rooted in all levels of society.[60] Gifts to churches and monasteries were regarded as service to the

---

[57] *Vita domni Willelmi Abbatis*, in Glaber, *Opera*, 272–3.
[58] Fauroux no. 199 (1051–1060).
[59] Orderic, iv. 90–3.
[60] Cassandra Potts, *Monastic Revival and Regional Identity in Early Normandy* (Woodbridge, 1997), ch. 3.

Plate 5   *Abbey of La Trinité, Caen – west front (Conway Library A64/77).*
By courtesy of the Conway Library, Courtauld Institute of Art.

saints who were their patrons and protectors. Many of these saints
had played a part in the evangelization of Normandy. Wherever
possible relics were brought back from the distant churches where
they had been taken during the Viking invasions. The ancient cults
were preserved in liturgy and pilgrimage, and this continuity of worship helped to secure the loyalty of the indigenous peasantry to their
new lords. Monasteries too helped to give security to the war-ravaged
districts on the frontiers of Normandy, and to encourage resettlement.
Combined with the ducal control over appointments, even in monasteries that had been privately founded, this helped to build a strong

regional identity. Once firm control had been extended on the frontier of Brittany to Mont-Saint-Michel, which had once looked as much to Breton as to Norman lords, an important step had been taken in building the unity and strength of the duchy of Normandy, and giving reality to the multi-racial Norman people throughout the whole of society.[61]

---

[61] Cassandra Potts, '"Atque unum ex diversis gentibus populum effecit": Historical tradition and the Norman identity', *ANS*, 18 (1996), 139–52.

Part II

Conquest and Settlement in the North

3

The Kingdom of England

The Norman conquest of England was the most carefully planned as well as the most remarkable of all the Norman enterprises. Good fortune may have played a small part: yet William of Poitiers had his finger on the truth when he wrote, comparing Duke William to Julius Caesar, that Caesar left too much to chance, whereas William prepared for all eventualities.[1] To transport a large army with horses and equipment across the Channel meant bringing together nearly a thousand ships as well as knights, archers and foot-soldiers; training the men and horses; organizing supplies for several weeks without ravaging his own lands, deceiving Harold about his intentions, being ready to land whenever and wherever the English coast was least guarded (Caesar had once been repulsed by British forces on the shore), and ensuring that men and horses were in a fit state to fight a major battle against a strong army very soon after reaching England. Inevitably there was an element of chance: a Norman victory would have been very difficult if not impossible had Harold not been forced to hurry to Yorkshire to fight off an invasion from another claimant to the English throne, King Harald Hardrada of Norway, accompanied by Harold Godwineson's exiled and disgruntled brother Tostig. But William must have known of the Norwegian threat, even if he was unsure when he finally put to sea whether the army that would face him would be English or Norwegian. He waited, first for four weeks at the mouth of the Dives and then at Saint-Valery-sur-Somme, spreading stories that he was waiting for a favourable wind; he did not finally embark for crossing until the English fleet had withdrawn from the

[1] William of Poitiers, II. 39, 40, p. 172.

Channel and Harold had hurried north to face and defeat the invaders at Stamford Bridge. At first, when the fleet was being assembled at the mouth of the Dives, William may have contemplated crossing to Hampshire; but it is far more likely that his strategy was to keep Harold's forces strung out along the coast, uncertain where the blow would fall, and to prefer a shorter crossing to a coast well known to the monks of his abbey at Fécamp. They had lands in Sussex, and were familiar with the harbours and the immediate hinterland; they provided one of his boats, and one monk at least accompanied the army.[2]

William's army waited for two weeks at Saint-Valery, before seizing a moment when a crossing would be possible. Certainly a very favourable wind was a *sine qua non* in an enterprise on this scale; and William, anxious to show that his claim was favoured by God no less than the Pope, offered public prayers for divine protection with his whole army. Yet, as Pierre Bouet has pointed out, it is noteworthy that the favourable wind described by William of Poitiers and Guy of Amiens blew just three days after Harold's victory over Hardrada in Yorkshire had annihilated one invading army.[3] Once in England providing for the army ceased to be an immediate problem for Duke William, as the Normans were able to ravage Harold's lands in Sussex. The strategy had a dual purpose, since it compelled Harold to hurry south and face the Norman forces in a pitched battle, without waiting to assemble the military resources of the whole kingdom. The risks were many, but they were calculated risks.

Not least of the hazards was the challenge of the battle itself. Battle was, to the Normans as it had been to the Romans, something only to be faced if all else failed.[4] Offensive warfare was conducted mostly in sieges, accompanied by small skirmishes and systematic ravaging of the enemy's country. In 1066, however, there was no possibility of retreat. The only sure way of disposing of a rival claimant was to defeat and kill him in battle; even to capture and imprision him would be no more than an invitation to conspiracies and rebellions. This was all the more necessary when the opponent had been crowned king. The Norman army had to be trained and ready to meet an unknown enemy on a site probably chosen by him. This may well have been the chief reason for the long delay in Normandy before the embarkation.

[2]   William of Poitiers, pp. xxiv–xxvi, and II. 12.
[3]   Pierre Bouet, 'Hastings: la triomphe de la ruse normande', *Historia, Special*, no. 59 (Mai–Juin 1999), 54.
[4]   John Gillingham, 'William the Bastard at war', *Studies in Medieval History presented to R. Allen Brown*, ed. C. Harper-Bill, C. Holdsworth and J. L. Nelson, 141–58.

Plate 6   *The Bayeux Tapestry – the battle of Hastings: Duke William raises his helmet to show that he is alive. Charles Stothard's copy of the Tapestry, reproduced by kind permission of the Society of Antiquaries of London.*

But however well the diverse elements in the army had been trained by six weeks' practice to execute complicated manoeuvres on horseback in some kind of coordinated action, the greatest risk that William took was probably that of fighting in person (in accordance with normal Norman practice) in the thick of the battle. This was essential in order to keep up the morale of the army and to exercise some kind of control; but had be been killed the whole enterprise would have collapsed (plate 6).

William of Poitiers exaggerated when he claimed that Duke William conquered England in one battle.[5] But even though over three more years of campaigning were necessary to secure Norman rule, no one could deny that the battle fought a few miles north of Hastings on 14 October 1066 was decisive. In a grim, day-long struggle with heavy casualties, King Harold and his brothers Gyrth and Leofwin perished, and any centrally organized resistance to the Norman invader collapsed. In the face of a Norman army, advancing and living off the

[5]   William of Poitiers, II. 26, p. 142.

country with all the plundering this entailed, the surviving English leaders, including both archbishops, decided not to offer further resistance. Dover, Canterbury, and then London capitulated. On Christmas day 1066 Duke William was crowned in Edward the Confessor's church of Westminster, with the acclamations (whether willing or unwilling) of the English no less than the Normans. Thereafter he had the immense advantage of the Church's blessing; he dated his reign from that day. There was no convincing counter-claim to the throne; Edgar Atheling, of the English royal line, was young and inexperienced; not until 1069 was any attempt made (by rebels in the north) to put him forward as king, and by that time the Normans were too firmly entrenched. William had come claiming the throne by hereditary right, and professing to respect the just laws and customs of the kingdom. He took into his own hand the royal demesnes, the lands of the Godwine family and the lands of those who had fought against him at Hastings; but for a time he left others in possession of their estates. The risings of the next few years finally brought about a change in his plans; within twenty years almost the whole of the English aristocracy had been destroyed.[6]

The wealth of surviving English records, most notably the remarkable surveys recorded in Domesday Book, make it possible to see more clearly than in Italy or any other region occupied by the Normans the methods by which they gradually imposed their rule, while preserving many of the customs and institutions they found in the conquered country. The first essential was to tighten their military grip, while making the fullest possible use of the cooperation of the Church. Castles were an essential element in every stage of conquest. Castles of the motte and bailey type could be thrown up very quickly with the aid of forced labour; these were the bases for the Norman leaders with their own household troops to defend themselves and prepare for further advance. They made use of whatever materials were at hand. Most of the first structures were wooden; but substantial royal castles – palaces almost, such as the Tower of London and the remarkable castle at Colchester – took advantage of any stone available from dismantled Roman buildings.[7] A Norman motte could be erected within the walls of an existing fortified area, whether Roman or

[6] Ann Williams, *The English and the Norman Conquest* (Woodbridge, 1995), ch. 2; Robin Fleming, *Kings and Lords in Conquest England* (Cambridge, 1991), 109–14.

[7] R. A. Brown, H. M. Colvin and A. J. Taylor, *The King's Works*, I (London, 1963), 20–5; R. A. Brown, 'The castles of the Conquest', *Domesday Book Studies*, ed. A. Williams and R. W. H. Erskine (London, 1987), 65–71.

Anglo-Saxon, as the new fortifications at Pevensey and Dover showed. Orderic Vitalis summed up the situation when he wrote that, to meet the dangers from rebellions, King William 'rode to all the remote parts of his kingdom and fortified strategic sites against enemy attack. The fortifications called castles by the Normans were scarcely known in the English provinces, and so the English – in spite of their courage and love of fighting – could put up only a weak resistance to their enemies.' He added that 'William appointed strong men from his Norman forces as guardians of the castles, and distributed rich fiefs that induced men to endure toil and danger to defend them.'[8]

Orderic was writing of the first actions of the Normans after their victory. When William of Malmesbury later summed up in his vignette on the Normans the impact of a new, military aristocracy, he included much more than castle-building. He commented on the luxurious clothing and diet of the Normans. They were a people accustomed to fighting, scarcely knowing how to live without war: energetic in attacking an enemy and, when force did not prevail, equally able to triumph by guile and bribery. At home they created great buildings at moderate cost; emulous of their equals, they strove to outdo their betters and protect their clients from outsiders. Of all peoples they were the most ready to welcome newcomers, whom they treated with equal honour; and they intermarried with the conquered people.[9]

Both Orderic and William of Malmesbury later wrote reflectively of the Norman people. The first step, however, had been military occupation. William's army consisted of his own household troops and contingents of varying sizes contributed by his auxiliaries. His first acts were to secure his base by building castles at Pevensey and Hastings, and strengthening the fortifications at Dover. In these and in the other castles that he built he placed powerful vassals as castellans. To reward his followers and to ensure the support of a large permanent military force in England he distributed confiscated lands. Some of the greatest magnates received estates sufficient to support the troops they had brought in the ships they had supplied.[10] For some of his own men he made provision by insisting that monasteries and bishoprics supported them. One important factor determining the numbers demanded from individual churches was his need to keep troops ready for action in all the danger spots of his kingdom. These

---

[8]   Orderic, ii. 194–5, 218–19.
[9]   WMGR, ii. 306.
[10] E. M. C. van Houts, 'The ship-list of William the Conqueror', ANS, 10 (1987), 159–83.

included in particular the estuaries and marshes of East Anglia, open to attack from Danish invaders, and the West Country, threatened by the surviving members of the Godwine family, who had taken refuge in Ireland. Practical considerations were important in determining the large contingents of knights demanded from Glastonbury and Peterborough in particular.[11]

Map 3   *Castles built by William I or with his sanction, 1066–1071 (based on* The King's Works, i. 25)

[11]   M. Chibnall, *Anglo-Norman England 1066–1166* (Oxford, 1986), 30–2.

Plate 7   *Rochester castle. By courtesy of English Heritage.*

During the years 1066–9, when rebellions threatened the newly established Norman power, the armies continued to ravage along the campaign routes. William was learning how to make use of the existing administration with its sheriffs and collecting centres for taxes, and at the same time was making it clear to all that resistance would not be tolerated. Later he was able to make better arrangements for collecting stores along the routes taken by his armies, and even sometimes sending supplies by sea. At all times, however, castles were established or strengthened as he advanced. After the first rising in the West Country a castle was built at Exeter within the town walls.[12] A trail of castles was left along the route followed by his army as it

---

[12]   Orderic, ii. 210–15.

travelled north and west to suppress risings in Yorkshire and along the Welsh borders. The worst threat of all in 1068–9, when native unrest was accompanied by a Danish invasion, provoked savage reprisals. William's brutal harrowing of the north met with universal condemnation and left indelible memories.[13]

Chroniclers named only the principal royal castles (Plate 7); many other smaller castles were built at the administrative centres of estates granted to William's vassals. They provided the strong dwelling places of the Norman aristocracy, probably included by William of Malmesbury in the buildings he found noteworthy. Fortified centres equipped for defence, they were also places of residence, where the normal business of the lord's court could be carried on. They provided if need be bases for further advance, especially along the moving frontiers. Careful planning went into the distribution of lands to support the greater castles, especially in regions where danger most threatened.

The Normans who settled in England were always a minority, but from the first they were a dominant minority and their impact on the realm was considerable. Within twenty years all the most prominent secular magnates had been replaced by continentals, and only two pre-1066 bishops still survived: the Englishman Wulfstan of Worcester and the Lotharingian Giso of Wells. Earls, king's thanes and almost all the wealthiest thanes had either fallen in battle or fled into exile; one, Earl Waltheof of Northumbria, had suffered the English punishment of execution after being involved in rebellion for the second time. Edgar Atheling, hesitant at first, had allowed northern rebels to elect him ineffectually as king before the rising collapsed and he took refuge in Scotland. The bulk of the English and Anglo-Danish population, however, still remained. It included many thanes of moderate wealth, men such as reeves who had been involved in administration, prominent townsmen,[14] and valued craftsmen, in particular the goldsmiths. William took care to retain the men with the local knowledge and skills he needed to help him pick up the threads of administration; he was well aware that the English coinage was far superior to anything in Normandy or France.[15] The survival rate of landholders was highest in the north of England and the marches of Wales.[16] Some

---

[13]　Orderic, ii. 230–2.
[14]　Williams, *The English*, ch. 2; Paul Dalton, *Conquest, Anarchy and Lordship* (Cambridge, 1994), ch. 1.
[15]　M. Dolley, *The Norman Conquest and the English Coinage* (London, 1966); P. Nightingale, 'Some London moneyers in the eleventh and twelfth centuries', *The Numismatic Chronicle*, 142 (1982), 34–50.
[16]　Judith M. Green, *The Aristocracy of Norman England* (Cambridge, 1997), ch. 2.

members of once-wealthy families remained on a portion of their former estates. Some noble women conferred a form of legitimacy by marrying the invaders who received their family lands. And the Church retained the bulk of its landed wealth, sometimes after paying for restitution and undertaking the expense of supporting knights on church estates and providing garrisons to guard the new castles. Some of the monastic treasures, however, were plundered and given to churches in Normandy.

Like the Northmen who had built up a strong province in Normandy by preserving the older institutions of the region they had

Plate 8 *Bilingual charter of Odo, bishop of Bayeux, with drawing of seal, now lost. (Obv. equestrian figure with sword and shield; rev. the bishop standing, tonsured with crozier.) From Sir Christopher Hatton's* Book of Seals, Northamptonshire Record Society 15 (1950), plate VIII. *By kind permission of the Northamptonshire Record Society.*

conquered, the Normans established lasting rule by taking over much that they found in the Old English state. The difference was that England in 1066 was already a united kingdom with far more developed instruments of government than those that had remained in the battered Carolingian region of Neustria in 911. Again, the Norman dukes were the firmly established rulers of a wealthy, strongly governed duchy, not the leaders of war bands as Rollo and his companions had been. Experienced in the art of government, they took over the rule of a wealthy kingdom, and made the most of its remarkable potential. In doing so they ultimately lost their own identity; but, realists as they were, they enjoyed the power and wealth and preserved the myth.

They used experienced local agents at all levels to learn new skills from them and to carry on the work of government, sometimes with local modifications. The pre-Conquest rulers had used the Old English language rather than Latin in many of their instruments of government, whereas the Normans were accustomed to Latin. For a few years after 1066 they sometimes issued bilingual writs (plate 8); but from about 1070 the English language appeared only in a few documents with wide implications, which were likely to be read out in the shire courts.[17] While much spoken business in the king's court was in French, the new vernacular did not begin to appear in official documents until the late twelfth century. In the local courts, however, where oral testimony played a very important part and sworn juries of neighbours were involved, interpreters were essential to overcome the language barrier.[18] Knowledge of both English and French, in the Anglo-Norman form that was developing, became necessary for the local bailiffs and reeves. And the process of adaptation had to be very rapid indeed.

King William's claim to be the lawful successor of King Edward and the just preserver of the laws and customs of his new kingdom was not lightly made. Even though the redistribution of lands took place so quickly and even roughly that many new lords hardly knew what their properties were, those who believed themselves unjustly disinherited were entitled to lodge a claim for restitution. Hundreds availed themselves of the possibility; some even were successful.[19] The great churches led the way; and since some of their complaints

[17] *Regesta Regum Anglo-Normannorum. The Acta of William I (1066–1087)*, ed. David Bates (Oxford, 1998), 50–2.
[18] H. Tsurushima, 'Domesday interpreters', *ANS*, 18 (1996), 201–22.
[19] R. Fleming, *Domesday Book and the Law* (Cambridge, 1998), 74–5.

about dispossession went back before 1066 they had a good chance of success. They were not alone; numerous lesser lay landholders demanded justice. Their pleas were heard in local courts before king's representatives helped by sworn juries of neighbours, whose memories stretched back for a generation or more. Where pleas involved scattered properties joint sessions of men from several counties could be held; such assemblies were a legacy from before the conquest. Further evidence was provided by stewards of the greater estates. Men of this type had been useful agents before the Normans came; but their increased importance shows one way in which the Normans reinforced the strength of Anglo-Saxon kingship with customs of their own.

Lordship had been an essential part of ducal power in Normandy, and it was strengthened by the need to support the king in a country conquered on the battlefield. It brought changes, both visible and institutional: to the visible symbols of the castles was added the activity of the honorial courts. Pre-Conquest lords had sometimes had fortified dwellings, and many of the Norman tenants who took over modest estates set up their households in 'castles' that were little more than fortified manor houses.[20] Even Castle Acre in Norfolk, in spite of its impressive earthworks, has been described as 'a country house'.[21] But the numbers of such residences impressed the indigenous population and the chroniclers, who saw them as instruments and symbols of conquest; many, like Chilham Castle, in time improved their defences and became more sophisticated strongholds, useful in times of disorder and internal conflict (plate 9).[22]

Many castles played an important part in the process of colonization that followed rapidly in the wake of conquest. The combination of castle, monastery and borough, or of two of these elements (which already existed in Normandy) formed one of the chief instruments of Norman colonization in Britain.[23] It provided for military and spiritual needs, while stimulating economic life and setting up a market for the surrounding rural settlements. At Arundel, Lewes, Shrewsbury, Chepstow, Gloucester and Pontefract, for example, the combination

[20] A. Williams, 'A bell-house and a burh-geat: lordly residences in England before the Norman Conquest', *The Ideals and Practice of Medieval Knighthood*, 4, ed. C. Harper- Bill and R. Harvey (Woodbridge, 1992), 221–40.
[21] J. G. Coad and A. P. F. Streeten, 'Excavations at Castle Acre castle, Norfolk', *Archaeological Journal*, 139 (1982), 138–301. William d'Aubigny's castle at Castle Rising was similar in purpose to Castle Acre.
[22] R. Allen Brown, *Castles from the Air* (Cambridge, 1989), 85–6.
[23] Le Patourel, *NE*, 317.

Plate 9 *William d'Aubigny's castle of Castle Rising.*

of these elements helped to sustain frontier defence, often combined with preparations for further advances. William I established his vassals in the marches of Wales, pushing on along the shore of the Bristol Channel to St Davids, but merely looking across the sea to Ireland. His son William Rufus continued to encourage a drive into northern Wales, as well as advancing in the north of England and consolidating his hold on Carlisle. Further advances and colonization took a different shape in both Wales and Scotland and ultimately in Ireland. But by the time William Rufus's sudden death in a hunting accident in 1100 had opened the way for the succession of Henry I, the Norman settlement in England was moving into a new phase.

Changes in the first decades of the twelfth century illustrate the way in which the Normans had adapted to their new status in a new country. The changes were slow and patchy, and varied from region to region. The main trend was to turn the Normans consciously into English. It can be seen particularly in the application of the law and in reforms of the Church.

When William the Conqueror set in motion the great survey that was to produce Domesday Book and accelerated the number of cases resulting from claims of dispossession, he also summoned an assembly to Salisbury and (it has been suggested) took oaths of fealty from both tenants and sub-tenants to secure their tenure of the lands granted to them at various times and in various ways.[24] This was an expression of the Norman administration of law, which involved an enormous

---

[24] J. C. Holt, '1086', in *Domesday Studies*, ed. J. Holt (Woodbridge, 1987), 41–64.

increase in the amount of business coming into the king's court. It was part of the process by which the royal court, which had been active in the king's business before 1066, increased in addition the number of writs issued there to initiate pleas between tenants, while still preserving and encouraging the lords' courts. This resulted from the powerful lordship of an effective conqueror imposed on a sophisticated system of administration that already existed. As Robin Fleming suggested, the adjudication and resolution of disputes at the inquest 'may have been a first step towards the genesis of a new streamlined lordship in England, which more tightly bound together personal, jurisdictional and territorial lordship, collapsing them into the compact honorial rights that were to become ubiquitous in the twelfth century'.[25] This was done by slowly modifying and adapting, but not destroying, the ancient laws and customs of England.

In the half-century after Henry I promised in his coronation charter to restore 'the laws of King Edward together with those emendations which my father made with the counsel of his barons',[26] a number of anonymous writers compiled collections claiming to record some at least of these laws. Very popular at the time, dismissed as forgeries unworthy of credence from the seventeenth century until the twentieth, they are now recognized as having historical value. If handled critically they can indicate the customs prevailing in different regions of England during the period of slow adaptation to a changing law. The earliest of these, the *Leges Henrici Primi*,[27] was produced probably between 1113 and 1118. The author used the Anglo-Saxon law codes up to the time of Cnut, and thereafter such of the scattered legal enactments as were known to him. It was an honest, if unsystematic and disordered attempt to show the law as it existed in his own time. A later collection, the *Leges Edwardi Confessoris*, was most probably compiled about 1140, certainly before 1150. Because of its manifestly false assertion that 'four years after the acquisition of England' King William 'caused to be summoned wise men learned in the law, twelve from each county, to swear to declare the rules of their laws and customs to the best of their ability', it was dismissed as a forgery in the seventeenth century, and has only recently begun to be regarded as a potentially useful source of information. It never attempted to be comprehensive, as it was particularly concerned with the peace of God and Holy Church, the king's peace, and methods of enforcing the

[25] Fleming, *Domesday Book*, 74–5.
[26] William Stubbs, *Select Charters*, 9th edn (Oxford, 1929), 116–19.
[27] *Leges Henrici Primi*, ed. L. J. Downer (Oxford, 1972), 34–7.

peace. In addition, it related particularly to a region in the North Midlands and Yorkshire, on the borders of the Danelaw. The author stressed continuity with pre-Conquest England, even claiming (possibly with some justification) that a murder fine had first been introduced under Cnut and revived under Edward the Confessor. At the same time he was aware of regional differences of custom and practice, and illustrated, sometimes unconsciously, changes in the laws of sanctuary, the extension of the king's peace, and the workings of the surety system. In Bruce O'Brien's telling phrase, the author 'catches and freezes some law in motion'.[28] What is striking in the history of the Norman people is the determination of recent settlers, employed almost certainly in the administration of the kingdom, to identify themselves with the English. Their treatises show how, during almost a century of adaptation, the slowly emerging common law was not just a mixture or a compound of two old national laws; it was different from what had previously existed in either country or would have emerged if the Conquest had never taken place.[29]

Similarly the Normans adopted and modified the customs, institutions and cults of the English Church during the same period. As in Normandy these were an important means of acculturation at all levels of society. In spite of many local differences and some local friction the English Church as a whole was never associated with any rebellion against the Normans. This was partly because William had come as a self-avowed reformer, with a record of reform in the Norman Church and the approval of the pope behind him. When Archbishop Stigand and two English bishops were removed from their sees in 1070 they were accused, not of political misconduct or sedition, but of simony and other ecclesiastical crimes and condemned in a church council.[30] Other sees were given to Normans only after the incumbents had died. The men who replaced them were on the whole reformers: most conspicuously, Lanfranc of Bec was chosen as archbishop of Canterbury. He became the mainstay of reform and brought in many Norman prelates, ostensibly not because of opposition to Englishmen, but because they were familiar with the reforming canons promulgated in Norman church councils. Changes of this kind would have come to England in time; the Conquest speeded up the change.

[28]   Bruce O'Brien, *God's Peace and King's Peace: The Laws of Edward the Confessor* (Philadelphia, 1999).
[29]   F. Pollock and F. W. Maitland, *The History of English Law before the Time of Edward I*, 2nd edn, 2 vols (Cambridge, 1968), i. 80.
[30]   'The Legatine Council at Winchester', *Councils and Synods*, ed. D. Whitelock, M. Brett, C. N. L. Brooke, I. 2 (Oxford, 1981), 565–74.

The Normans were lavish in their church endowments. New wealth gave them the means, and the violence by which it had been won made them open to suggestions that they ought to make atonement for their share in the slaughter of battle. In 1070 penitential ordinances were promulgated by the papal legate Ermenfrid of Sion. They prescribed suitable penances by way of expiation; gifts to churches and the founding of new religious houses were encouraged.[31] While the story later told in Battle Abbey that William the Conqueror had vowed on the field of battle to found an abbey on the spot where Harold had fallen may not be literally true, he certainly began his new foundation within a few years of his victory. In spite of protests that a hilltop site was unsuitable because of the need for a convenient water supply, once his mind was set on the project he insisted that his new abbey must stand on the battlefield and that the difficulties must be overcome. His work in stimulating monastic life as king of England was not quite the same as his earlier work in Normandy, for England already had a number of wealthy and ancient abbeys; and moreover increasing papal power and influence meant that he had to share the role of guardian of the Church's peace. But he showed himself ready to protect loyal churches, confirm their possessions and privileges, and distribute endowments. There was never any suggestion that his place of burial should be anywhere but in the abbey of Saint-Étienne that he had founded in Caen, near his wife's chosen burial place in her abbey of La Trinité. Place of death sometimes determined place of burial and he died in Normandy, but there is no reason to suppose that death in England would have led to burial at Battle, much less in Edward the Confessor's church at Westminster, which did not become a royal mausoleum until the thirteenth century.

His magnates quickly followed his example. Relatively few independent abbeys were founded; one problem was the need to procure monks for a new community, and the Norman and French abbeys who provided the monks were usually reluctant to relinquish their control over the new houses. Marmoutier, which provided monks for Battle after the abbot of Cluny had refused to send any, resisted the independence of the house at first. Sées made half-hearted attempts to keep a share in the election of abbots in Roger of Montgomery's foundation at Shrewsbury. Chester, where Earl Hugh founded an abbey in the church of St Werburgh, had no such problem; Anselm willingly sent monks from Bec, but did not wish to undertake responsibility for

---

[31] Ibid., 563–4, 581–4.

Plate 10   *Cluniac priory of Wenlock, Shropshire, founded by Roger of Montgomery. Fragment of carving from the lavabo, showing Christ calling Peter (c.1182), with Cluniac influence (Conway Library A84/767). By courtesy of the Conway Library, Courtauld Institute of Art.*

discipline in a house so far away once the community was well established. Cluny was better organized to provide new colonies under a loose control readily accepted by the benefactors. Once the Normans were firmly established in England the abbots were more willing to send their monks overseas; by 1077 William of Warenne and his wife Gundrada were able to found the first Cluniac house in England at Lewes; and their son William earl of Surrey brought Cluniac monks to Castle Acre in Norfolk a decade later. They were the first of many (plate 10). Most benefactors gave modest gifts to support small communities from their family abbeys in Normandy; these retained their allegiance and formed the group later known as the alien priories. A number were castle priories, established at the *caput* of an honour; their foundation was part of the Norman process of colonization and settlement. Their size and importance varied with the wealth and power of their patrons, who ranged from the lords of Clare, founders of Stoke-by-Clare as a Bec dependency, to Manasses Arsic, who had replaced Odo of Bayeux's vassal Wadard at Cogges in Oxfordshire and established a tiny cell of Fécamp there.[32]

The direction of Norman church endowments shifted towards the end of the eleventh century, with a greater number of gifts going to English houses. Some had received new donations before the death of William the Conqueror. Gloucester, a poor abbey in 1066, profited from its strategic position as a gateway to Wales, and from the frequent presence of the royal court for seasonal crown-wearings until these were abandoned by Henry I. Both king and magnates contributed new endowments. St Albans was favoured by Archbishop Lanfranc, and the appointment of his able and energetic nephew Paul as abbot in 1077 marked the beginning of a flood of gifts. Both these houses, together with Durham, were unusual in attracting newly founded dependent priories, endowed by prominent Normans who were committed to a future in England. Some, like William d'Aubigny, founder of Wymondham priory in Norfolk as a cell of St Albans, made provision in their charters for the house to become independent if the endowment increased sufficiently; but the grip of the mother abbeys was usually tight, and independence was rarely achieved.[33]

The pattern of monastic endowment shows that many Normans were settling in England and establishing branches of their families in the lands they had acquired there. It was part of the process of anglicization. New monastic orders soon attracted considerable endowments, though the older Benedictines did not lose the support of families connected in one way or another with the houses. The Cistercians in particular attracted numerous postulants, and their organization ensured that a new community of monks would be provided and subsequently controlled by a mother-house. But new men who had acquired wealth and lands by administrative or military service began to settle as country gentlemen and aspiring benefactors, and looked more and more to the regular canons. Some

---

[32] See in general David Knowles, *The Monastic Order in England 943–1216*, 2nd edn (Cambridge, 1966); Emma Cownie, *Religious Patronage in Anglo-Norman England 1066–1135* (Woodbridge and Rochester, NY, 1998); Frank Barlow, *The English Church 1066–1154* (London, 1979).

[33] M. Chibnall, 'Le Problème des réseaux monastiques en Angleterre', *Piety, Power and History in Medieval England and Normandy* (repr. Variorum Series, Ashgate, 2000), no. V.

new foundations grew out of small hermitages; some attracted war-weary knights. The Augustinians found royal favour also; both Henry I and his wife Matilda were patrons of Augustinian houses. When Henry I established a new bishopric at Carlisle to strengthen his grip on the northern frontier, he set up a cathedral chapter of Augustinian canons. Indeed the order appealed to him so much that in Normandy too he chose Augustinian canons to replace secular canons in the cathedral chapter of Sées.

All these benefactors looked to the houses in their patronage for both spiritual and temporal gains. They valued the prayers of the monks, and saw clearly that the estates of their monasteries increased the scope and permanence of their authority. Many chose burial in the abbeys or priories they regarded as their own. In these houses and their parish churches they adopted any saints who had a strong local cult, alongside the saints of the universal calendar and an occasional saint, like St Lo (St Laud) of Coutances, who had been their protector in Normandy. Here, as in Normandy, the fostering of local cults helped to strengthen the roots of Norman power.

Initially some were reluctant to accept English saints of whom they had never heard. This problem had not existed for Rollo and other early leaders, converted from paganism and ready to find their patrons among the apostles and holy men and women of the region they had conquered. At first Lanfranc, who was in his own words 'a new Englishman', found the proliferation of cults of saints totally unknown to him bewildering, particularly as he was in touch with movements in the Church towards stricter criteria for canonization. Persuaded by his friend Anselm, abbot of Bec and later his successor as archbishop of Canterbury, he became more receptive. Within thirty years of the Conquest the Norman abbots were willingly taking up the defence of the English saints associated with their churches. Anselm even carried away to Normandy a relic of St Neot, patron of one of Bec's daughter-houses in England, and so established an enduring cult at Bec. King William for his part reinforced his authority by promoting the cult of powerful royal saints. In this he was ably seconded by one of the few continental prelates to survive the conquest: Baldwin, abbot of Bury St Edmunds and former monk of Saint-Denis, who vigorously promoted the cult of St Edmund in Normandy and further afield.[34]

---

[34] S. J. Ridyard '*Condigna veneratio*: post-Conquest attitudes to the saints of the Anglo-Saxons', *ANS*, 9 (1987), 179–206; P. A. Hayward, 'Translation narratives in post-Conquest hagiography and English resistance to the Norman Conquest', *ANS*, 21 (1999), 67–93.

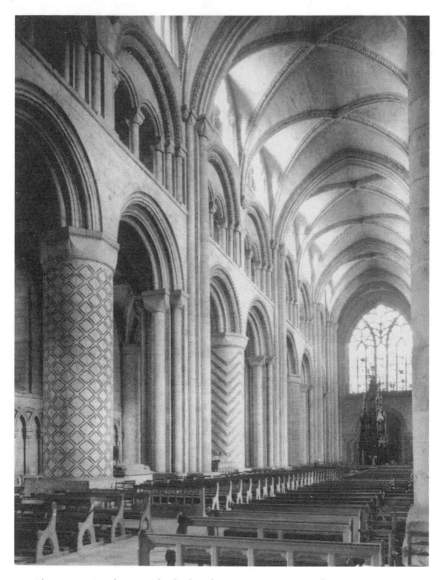

Plate 11   *Durham cathedral – the nave (Conway Library A61/559).*
By courtesy of the Conway Library, Courtauld Institute of Art.

As William of Malmesbury observed, these new bishops and abbots
were great builders. They rebuilt their cathedrals and abbeys on a
grand scale and in a new style (plates 11 and 12). The removal of
cherished shrines provoked resentment in some places. Eadmer of

Plate 12   *Church of Waltham Holy Cross – the nave, showing influence of Durham (Conway Library A86/6558). By courtesy of the Conway Library, Courtauld Institute of Art.*

Canterbury, the companion and biographer of Anselm, looked with regret at the passing of the England he had known, even while resisting (as his revered master had done) any attempt at lay investiture.

Table 2　The Norman kings of England (simplified)

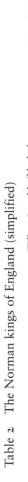
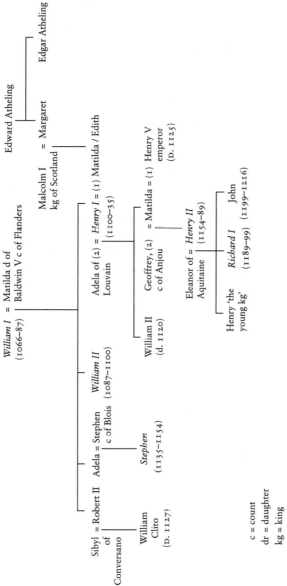

Enough was retained for many Englishmen to accept the changes; intermarriage further mixed the peoples, and within a hundred years of the Conquest it had become difficult to separate Norman and English influences in the new culture. Writers still referred to Normans and English; but the terms no longer meant the same as in the immediate aftermath of 1066.[35]

Because personal lordship was of great importance during the period of Norman expansion and settlement, questions of inheritance and the division of property remained crucial long after new and more permanent instruments of government had taken shape. William the Conqueror was king of England and duke of Normandy; he did not enjoy exactly the same authority in both parts of his realm. No precedent existed to determine the form in which they should be passed on to his heirs. Events forced his hand to some extent, and his choice was limited when he lay on his death-bed in 1087. Robert, his eldest son, had quarrelled with his father, made common cause with the king of France, and gone into exile in 1083; yet Robert had been designated as heir to Normandy before 1066, and had in all probability been made duke in association with his father afterwards. He could not be overlooked. The next son, William Rufus, became king of England by his father's wish.[36] The youngest, Henry, received nothing except his mother's lands in Normandy; yet he succeeded in seizing the crown after the sudden death of William Rufus, and in the course of time forced his brother Robert to relinquish Normandy. Robert ended his days in captivity, and his only son was driven into exile and predeceased him. Henry himself had only one legitimate son, William, and there should have been no succession problem in either the kingdom of England or the duchy of Normandy, still held in an ill-defined way by the king of France. But in 1120 young William was drowned in the *White Ship*, and the succession became complicated by the question of female inheritance. Although the Norman barons were prepared to acknowledge Henry's widowed daughter, the empress Matilda, as his heir, the position of her second husband, Geoffrey count of Anjou, was never clarified. The result was a disputed succession after Henry's nephew Stephen of Blois seized the throne of England and was accepted by the French king as duke of Normandy.

---

[35] See below, pp. 111–12.

[36] R. H. C. Davis, 'William of Jumièges, Robert Curthose and the Norman succession', *EHR*, 95 (1986), 597–606; repr. *idem, From Alfred the Great to Stephen* (London and Rio Grande, 1991), 131–40; E. Z. Tabuteau, 'The rule of law in the succession to Normandy and England, 1087', *Haskins Society Journal* (1991), 141–69.

Plate 13 *Capital from the Angevin priory church of Cunault, showing an armed soldier (Conway Library B89/1155). By courtesy of the Conway Library, Courtauld Institute of Art.*

Civil war followed; Stephen lost Normandy to Geoffrey of Anjou, failed to secure the succession for his own son, and reluctantly accepted Matilda's son Henry as his heir. By the time Henry succeeded to the throne in 1154 he had been recognized as duke of Normandy and after his father's death as count of Anjou (plate 13).[37] He had also married Eleanor of Aquitaine, the divorced former wife of King Louis VII, who brought Henry her vast inheritance in the south of France. Norman elements in the realms governed by the heirs of the

[37] One of Young Henry's first official appearances in Anjou was in 1144 as witness to a charter concerning military service due from the Priory of Cunault (J. Chartrou, *L' Anjou de 1109 à 1151*, Paris, 1928, no. 149).

first dukes of Normandy became submerged in the so-called 'Angevin empire'.

At the same time there were important structural changes in government. Rouen had been the prosperous and thriving metropolis of the Norman duchy, equalling or surpassing Paris in its wealth and influence.[38] Inevitably as government became more settled and centralized the royal administration gravitated towards London. As long as the chief royal officers and the royal curia travelled with the king the relation between London and Rouen could remain undefined. Rouen could be hailed by poets as a new Rome, with imperial aspirations.[39] But by the end of the twelfth century Rouen was on the way to becoming a provincial capital, while London was the capital of a kingdom regarded by contemporaries as the realm of England.

Up to the middle of the twelfth century, however, Norman traditions remained strong in the territories that historians have called either 'the Norman empire' or 'the Anglo-Norman realm'. Moreover, it was a realm whose frontiers were still capable of expansion. It was also able to command the allegiance of other lordships beyond the frontiers, and to send out settlers into other kingdoms and principalities. Wales, Scotland and Ireland all received Norman settlers and were drawn into association with the Norman kings of England in different ways.

---

[38] Bernard Gauthiez, 'Paris, un Rouen capétien? Développements comparés de Rouen et Paris sous les règnes de Henri II et Philippe-Auguste', *ANS*, 16 (1994), 117–36.
[39] C. H. Haskins, *Norman Institutions* (Cambridge, Mass., 1925), 144–5.

4

Wales, Scotland, Ireland

Of the kingdoms and principalities bordering on England, Wales was the most vulnerable to Norman penetration and ultimately conquest. That the conquest took more than two hundred years to complete was due partly to Norman methods of settlement, partly to the geographical and political condition of the region. Norman advance into most parts of Europe and the Near East took the form of piecemeal settlement and the establishment of lordships under powerful military leaders. By defeating Harold and winning the English crown William the Conqueror took over a kingdom with well-developed instruments of government and claims to wider lordship over a number of neighbouring princes. It was not entirely clear where the frontiers should be drawn, or what kind of authority Edward the Confessor and his predecessors might have exercised beyond them. Even in the northern provinces of England the Normans were gradually feeling their way into Cumbria and Northumberland. They were prepared to test their claims and press them to the limit.

The position in Wales was unusually favourable.[1] In 1063 Gruffudd ap Llywelyn, the Welsh prince who had established a remarkable personal hegemony in Wales, was killed by his own men, and the region became a prey to the rivalries and feuds of warring princelings. In the same year Harold Godwineson led a successful campaign in a series of lightning raids that further dented Welsh authority; possibly he also brought part of south-east Wales under his direct lordship. Besides this, the later Anglo-Saxon kings had successfully asserted a form of overlordship over the Welsh princes. William I and his barons

[1] R. R. Davies, *Conquest, Coexistence and Change: Wales 1062–1415* (Oxford, 1987), esp. ch. 2; David Walker, *The Normans in Britain* (Oxford, 1995), ch. 3.

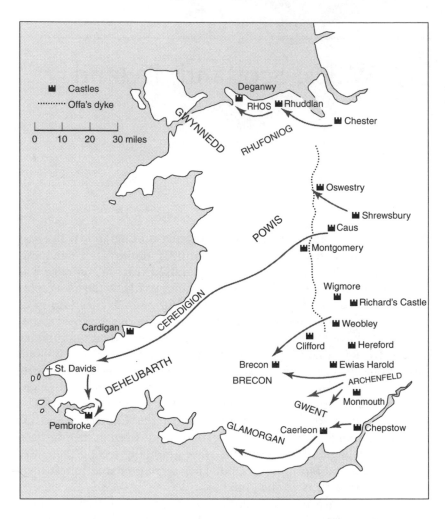

Map 4 *The advance into Wales (based on William Rees,* A Historical Atlas of Wales, *London, 1972, plates 29 and 30)*

lost no time in pressing their claims as well as beginning a process of gradual colonization and settlement.

The first task was to establish strong marcher lordships under King William's most trusted and masterful followers. By 1071 at latest earldoms had been created for Hugh of Avranches in Chester, Roger of Montgomery in Shrewsbury and William fitz Osbern in Hereford. Their task was both to prevent Welsh inroads across the frontier and to establish their influence among the Welsh princes. Initially this may have stopped short of a licence to conquer; but certainly campaigns into the Welsh territories were encouraged. These were most vigorous in south-east Wales; and although William fitz Osbern lost his life in 1071 during a brief adventure in Flanders he had established a pattern for future settlement.

As elsewhere, conquest was based on castles which, apart from his own mighty fortress in Chepstow, were held by his retainers and vassals. Their main purpose was to secure the surrounding lands for profitable exploitation. The familiar Norman pattern of castle, borough, and priory or abbey soon appeared along the coastal plain from Chepstow to Caerleon. The marcher lords did not, however, work in isolation, for King William pressed his claim to overlordship over Caradog ap Gruffudd. After Caradog's death in battle in 1081, King William led an expedition to treat with Rhys ap Tewdyr, who agreed to render £40 annually. William also advanced as far as St Davids, and on his return fortified a castle at Cardiff, where a mint was set up. Robert Fitzhamon was established in Cardiff, probably to maintain the Norman presence; after 1093, as royal authority weakened, Fitzhamon assumed control.[2]

The Norman presence in southern Wales was secured, not simply by initial seizure of power, but by steady colonization. The castles, boroughs and churches were focal points; settlers moved in to exploit the agricultural lands dependent on the castle. Some were Norman, but a great many were English. In Henry I's reign an alien group of Flemings, driven from their home, were brought into Pembrokeshire. They came in groups under military leaders, some of whom lent their names to settlements such as Wiston and Letterston.[3] A great many more settlers were English or Norman or the children of mixed marriages. In lowland Pembroke, Gower, Glamorgan, Gwent and some other border districts, 'the Norman conquest of Wales was accompanied and underpinned by extensive peasant colonisation', which began in the late eleventh century. There was some cultural assimilation, which worked both ways. This was perhaps the area most characteristic of Norman lordship, which attempted to bring different peoples into one nation and tried, not always successfully, to extend the ducal or royal protection through all levels of society. In this the contribution of the Church was important. Although some new churches were dedicated in the names of the early apostles and martyrs, many local cults were

[2] *Royal Commission on Historical Monuments. Glamorgan*, III, Part 1ᵃ (1991), 9–10.
[3] I. W. Rowlands, 'Aspects of the Norman settlement in Dyfed', *ANS*, 3 (1981), 142–57.

preserved, and the relics of local saints were eagerly collected to attract pilgrims to the rebuilt cathedrals.

The Normans had in fact taken over the English claims both to secular lordship over all the princes of Wales and to control of the Church. Just as the royal power of the first three Norman kings was essential to uphold the authority of the marcher lords, so the Church of Canterbury pressed the authority that it had begun to claim before the Conquest over the whole Church in Wales. The restructuring of the Welsh Church was to some extent part of the reform spreading through the whole of western Europe; but it was hastened by the coming of the Normans. Earlier Welsh bishops had exercised authority over scattered communities with no clear territorial or hierarchical structure. The Normans from the first pressed the authority of Canterbury. Lanfranc and Anselm both insisted that the metropolitan authority of their church extended over the whole of Wales. From the time that Urban was made bishop of Llandaff in 1107 newly appointed bishops made their professions of obedience to Canterbury. Even when political authority in Wales was shaken by revolt and no strong royal power was able to hold rebels in check (as during Stephen's reign), the bishops continued to accept the implications of their submission to Canterbury and this involved submission to the king. They swore fealty and attended royal councils. A short-lived attempt by Bernard, bishop of St Davids from 1115 to 1148, to urge the claim of his see to metropolitan status met with no success. When in 1188 Baldwin, archbishop of Canterbury, travelled through Wales to preach the crusade, he celebrated Mass without opposition in all four Welsh cathedrals. After 1203 even Gerald of Wales, the most vociferous advocate of the metropolitan status of St Davids, gave up the struggle. The way was being prepared for the final conquest of Wales by Edward I.[4]

Long before that time the stage had been reached when later historians would describe the descendants of the Normans in Wales as 'Anglo-Norman' or even 'English'. Only in the later eleventh and early twelfth centuries was it possible to consider the colonization and settlement as a movement of the 'Norman people'. By conquering England they had taken part in an enterprise that was to change their character and help to form a new 'English people'. Further advances, even when carried out by men of Norman descent, were to take place in part at least as an extension of the royal power, not as simply the limited enterprises of individual lords or earls.

[4]   Davies, *Conquest*, ch. 7.

In Scotland the Norman infiltration took a totally different form.[5] There was a strong Scots monarchy; and although William I and his sons secured some form of oath of allegiance or even homage in the marches from the Scots kings the relationship remained vague. It was further confused by the fact that the kings acquired an English earldom in Huntingdon. Although early wars were fought to define the frontiers of the two kingdoms, Norman settlers who moved into Scotland came by royal favour and invitation. They entered as kinsfolk, dependants or servants, not as conquerors. Scotland has been called a land of opportunity for younger sons. Skilled fighting men were needed and could hope for both land and office: the most conspicuously successful were the fitz Alans, descendants of the steward of Scotland, who fathered the line of Stuart kings. Ties of friendship were strengthened by the marriage of Henry I to Edith/Matilda, daughter of King Malcolm Canmore and Queen Margaret of Scotland, which led to Margaret's sons being welcomed at the English court. David, the youngest, grew up there, little expecting ever to become king. He had been given the earldom of Huntingdon by Henry I and had taken active part in the affairs of the kingdom before he succeeded to the throne of Scotland on the death of his elder brother Alexander in 1125. Possibly through contacts with the court and in Normandy he became an admirer of the Augustinian canons and the stricter monastic orders. Meeting Bernard of Tiron probably influenced his decision to bring a community of monks from Tiron to the abbey he was founding at Kelso. In any case the reformed orders were spreading throughout western Europe. Similarly, although Norman families such as the Morevilles or the fitz Alans came as vassals and feudal dependants, feudal tenures were not peculiar to Normandy; they were characteristic of many parts of western Europe. When Graeme Ritchie was writing of the Normans in Scotland, he coined the phrase 'Duke William's Breton, Lotharingian, Flemish, Picard, Artesian, Cenomanian, Angevin, general-French and Norman Conquest';[6] and though this was a racial blend that early Norman chroniclers proudly proclaimed as a characteristic of the Norman people, it tended to lose any ethnic unity it might have suggested when mingled with the other peoples among whom the Normans settled. In Scotland the new aristocracy that gradually infiltrated into the kingdom 'fitted in beside the old'. New lordships owing feudal services were gradually created

---

[5]   G. W. S. Barrow, *The Anglo-Norman Era in Scottish History* (Oxford, 1980); Walker, *Normans*, ch. 4.
[6]   R. L. G. Ritchie, *The Normans in Scotland* (Edinburgh, 1954), 157.

out of royal demesne to provide an aristocracy of service. The greatest
vassals became hereditary officers. Yet it is not surprising that the
twelfth century should have been described as 'the Anglo-Norman era
in Scottish history'. The new settlers illustrate the acculturation of the
Normans in a new society; in this sense only did they carry on the
history of the Norman people.

The Church was never effectively under the control of an English
metropolitan, though archbishops of York sometimes consecrated
bishops of St Andrews. Glasgow, from the twelfth century, looked for
a direct relationship with the papacy. A bond with the pope was
strengthened from 1192, when the independence of the Scottish Church
was given papal recognition, though Scotland remained without a
metropolitan for nearly three more centuries.[7] In this way, although
individual settlers from the Anglo-Norman realm hastened the introduction of new political and ecclesiastical structures, they were often
merely the instruments of much wider European movements.

Norman settlement in Ireland came later and in a different form.[8] It
too showed the effect that the conquest of a kingdom had had on the
Norman people. The first colonizing families who moved in from
1169, and more fully from 1172 when Henry II took the initiative,
were Anglo-Norman rather than Norman. There was also a strong
Welsh element in the families from southern Wales, who were to play a
major role in Ireland. The early relations of the Irish bishops with
archbishops Lanfranc and Anselm were little more than personal and
advisory; Lanfranc readily agreed to consecrate Irish bishops, but no
subsequent attempt was made to bring the Irish Church under the
metropolitan control of Canterbury. The establishment of archbish-
oprics at Dublin, Tuam, Armagh and Cashel owed more to papal than
to Norman influence; and early monastic foundations resulted from
direct contact with continental reformers. St Malachy was particularly
active in promoting the spread of Arrouaisian and Savigniac houses in
Ireland, and through his influence Mellifont became the parent monastery of a group of Cistercian houses.

Among earlier secular contacts, Arnulf of Montgomery married the
daughter of an Irish king and took refuge in Ireland for a time after
Henry I expelled the Bellême family from his realm. There was, however, no serious settlement before Henry II's reign. Then a small group
of families from south Wales began to intervene in the struggles of

[7] Walker, *Normans*, 80–2.
[8] Robin Frame, *Colonial Ireland* (Dublin, 1981), 7–19; Walker, *Normans*, ch. 5.

Plate 14 *Trim castle – gate-house and keep.*

Irish high kings in Leinster. Anglo-Norman troops began arriving in 1170, led by Richard fitz Gilbert, earl of Strigoil and his constable Hervey de Montmorency. Henry II, after at first opposing Earl Richard's independent action, sought papal approval and himself took the initiative. His invasion resulted in the establishment of Earl Richard (known as Strongbow) in Leinster and Hugh de Lacy in Meath. Both Strongbow and Hugh married into Irish royal families, and so sank their roots a little deeper. They were, however, holders of large fiefs under the English crown. Much of the actual colonization in Ireland took place in typically Norman fashion, with the principal magnates building castles (plate 14) and settling their vassals in numerous mottes scattered through the territories assigned to them.[9] These largely corresponded to existing divisions, and some elements of earlier Irish lordships were taken over by the newcomers. The obligations of knight-service, castle-guard and administrative office were, however, those they had known in England.[10] Moreover the initiative behind the conquest was royal, and by the late twelfth century legal

[9] T. E. McNeill, *Castles in Ireland: Feudal Power in a Gaelic World* (London and New York, 1997).
[10] M. T. Flanagan, 'Strategies of lordship in pre-Norman and post-Norman Leinster', *ANS*, 20 (1998), 107–26.

and administrative institutions were well established in England. The duties of royal tenants-in-chief were much more standardized than they had been a hundred years earlier. And, particularly after Henry II's son John arrived as prince of Ireland, Dublin became the centre of English administration and English law in Ireland. Justiciars were authorized to issue judicial writs on their own authority. Though the new lords were still often referred to as Normans they were in the process of becoming an Anglo-Norman aristocracy, very soon to be called English. In Ireland as elsewhere the Norman people became assimilated in new social structures, surviving only in antiquarian tradition and in myth.

Part III

The Normans in the South

5

Southern Italy

The Norman conquests in southern Italy began in much the same way as the first Scandinavian conquests in Neustria that led to the making of the duchy of Normandy. Overpopulation and bitter feuds or rebellions in Normandy drove many able men from landed families to seek their fortune elsewhere. With the difference that they had abandoned sea warfare and were trained to fight on horseback, they formed groups under an acknowledged leader for greater safety. Their urgent need was to support themselves, either as mercenaries in the armies of foreign princes or by plunder. Before long they began to demand land for settlement; then it was only a short step to expropriating their former allies and imposing their own rule.

Though the early stages may have been similar in both regions, the establishment of a duchy and in time a kingdom in south Italy took a very different course from the making of Normandy. Both the distribution of power and the social structure of the two regions were fundamentally different. One important common factor was the weakness of authority in both. In north-west France the battered Carolingian empire had crumbled, and the rulers were too weak to beat off repeated Viking invasions. In southern Italy the situation was far more complex, and the cultural divisions were more deeply rooted; but the lack of an effective central authority invited aggression in the same way.

Successive invasions had penetrated into Italy, transforming the administrative framework of the former Roman Empire and bringing in new dominant minorities without obliterating the indigenous peoples. The emperors in Constantinople still retained a foothold in the southern part of the peninsula, but Lombard rulers were established as far south as Apulia and Calabria, and the Greek administration was vigorous only in the extreme south-east. Moreover the Lombard states of Salerno, Benevento and Capua (formed out of the ancient duchy of Benevento) and the small duchies of Naples, Gaeta and Amalfi, though nominally subject to Constantinople, were virtually independent. They could form their own alliances and were involved in intermittent wars, both among themselves and against Saracen raiders along the coast. The whole of Sicily was in Saracen hands, though there too divisions existed between different powers. When the Normans appeared as mercenaries in the first decades of the eleventh century, the Greek government was making a recovery at the expense of Benevento and Salerno; and Norman pilgrims and adventurers were drawn in to help the Lombard population against the Greeks and occasionally to repel Saracen raiders. The situation gradually became further complicated by the conflicting claims to overlordship of both the Greek emperors and the reformed papacy.

Norman pilgrims returning from Jerusalem or the shrine of St Michael at Monte Gargano were drawn into local conflicts. Raoul Glaber tells how one group brought back to Normandy stories of a wealthy, war-torn country, where well-trained fighting men could earn good wages and enjoy a share in rich plunder.[1] Gradually war bands infiltrated into the country; before long they asked for land as a reward for their services. One of the earliest leaders, Rainulf Drengot, who appears to have been exiled from Normandy for some crime of violence, took service with Sergius IV, duke of Naples, against the prince of Capua. Whatever his status in Normandy may have been, he was described by Amatus of Monte Cassino as 'a man adorned with all the virtues appropriate for a knight'.[2] In 1028 Sergius settled Rainulf in Aversa, and gave him his own sister in marriage, thus legitimizing his position. Aversa was the earliest Norman settlement, from which further gains in Gaeta and Capua were possible. Before long there were others, particularly at Melfi. Here Norman leadership quickly passed into the hands of the family that was to consolidate Norman power, and ultimately to establish a kingdom in south Italy: the Hauteville family.

The Hautevilles were not rebels driven into exile; they were the sons of a landed vassal from the Cotentin, Tancred de Hauteville, whose modest estates were insufficient to support twelve sons. According to Geoffrey of Malaterra, Tancred himself was a remarkable warrior,

---

[1]   Glaber, III.3–4, pp. 96–103.
[2]   *Storia dei Normanni di Amato di Montecassino*, ed. V. de Bartholomeis (Fonti per la storia d'Italia, 13, Rome, 1935), p. 53.

whose exploits persuaded Richard II, duke of Normandy, to take him into his service and give him charge of a group of ten knights,[3] the characteristic (though not the invariable) unit of the Norman fighting forces. By his first wife he had five sons: William Iron Arm, Drogo, Humphrey, Geoffrey and Serlo; after her death his second wife, Fredesende, bore him seven more sons: Robert called Guiscard, Mauger, William, Alfred, Hubert, Tancred and Roger. All the young men were trained in the military arts, and were able to defend themselves and to attack an enemy. They agreed between themselves that their patrimony was too small to be shared, and so went off at various times to seek their fortune, leaving the paternal inheritance to one of the younger sons. Five of them were destined to become counts or dukes in south Italy, and to take part in building a kingdom where their descendants ruled until the end of the twelfth century.

The two older brothers, William Iron Arm and Drogo, began their careers by serving as mercenary leaders in the armies of various legitimate Lombard dukes, and sometimes of the Greek emperor. Both took part in an unsuccessful attempt by the emperor to win back Sicily from the Saracens. Once they had become more familiar with conditions in south Italy, they began to take over authority from the Greeks. William Iron Arm achieved unofficial status in Apulia with the approval of Count Gaimar IV of Salerno; and after his death in 1046 his brother Drogo was granted the title of 'Count of the Normans of all Apulia' by the western emperor Henry III. The brutality of the new Norman rulers, and their aggressiveness in Benevento, soon antagonized the pope no less than the Greeks and the western emperor. In 1053 Pope Leo IX was able to bring together a formidable army of German and Lombard forces to challenge the newcomers in the battle of Civitate. Among the Norman leaders the most conspicuous were Humphrey de Hauteville, his brother Robert Guiscard, and Richard count of Aversa. In spite of smaller numbers, their tactics (thanks to the force of their charge and their ability to manoeuvre and control their troops) won the day. The outcome was that the Normans made peace with Pope Leo, whom they had defeated, and received in turn his recognition of the possessions they had conquered and might conquer in the future, particularly in Sicily.

The account of the battle of Civitate in a long narrative poem by William of Apulia commented on the courage and skill of Humphrey, but gave the highest praise to Robert Guiscard, then at the beginning

---

[3] Malaterra, I. 40, p. 25.

of his career.[4] In time, with the assistance of his younger brother, Roger, he was to bring almost the whole of southern Italy under Norman control, and to lay the foundations of the future kingdom. His nickname, Guiscard ('the Wily'), was one that he accepted with pride: cunning, together with courage, eloquence, and authority, was a quality traditionally cherished by the Normans. The Greek princess, Anna Comnena, left a portrait of him as he was remembered by his enemies in her father's court:

> This Robert was a Norman by birth, of obscure origin, with an over-bearing character and a thoroughly villainous mind: he was a brave fighter, very cunning in his assaults on the wealth and power of great men; in achieving his ends absolutely inexorable, diverting criticism by incontrovertible argument. He was a man of immense stature...; he had a ruddy complexion, fair hair, broad shoulders, eyes that all but shot out sparks of fire.... In him all was admirably well-proportioned and elegant.[5]

Recalling Homer's comment that the shout of Achilles sounded like a multitude in uproar, she added, 'but Robert's bellow, so they say, put tens of thousands to flight.... He was no man's slave, owing obedience to nobody in the world.' William of Apulia wrote that he was called Guiscard because he surpassed Cicero in eloquence and Ulysses in cunning.[6]

Under Guiscard's leadership the Norman expansion in Italy became more clearly directed towards steady advance into Apulia and Calabria and ultimately towards winning power over the whole southern part of the peninsula and Sicily. Guiscard applied what had been learnt in his earlier career as a bandit and mercenary fighter. Since the Normans had come to Italy in small groups made up mostly of fighting men, they had adapted themselves to local conditions, taking over whatever they found valuable in each particular region, and often marrying into the most prominent local families. In the Lombard principalities they had found a kind of aristocracy, on which they imposed their power as counts. Apulia, however, had no true aristocracy and still preserved some vestiges of Byzantine administration based on walled towns. There was also a flourishing society of small

---

[4] Guillaume de Pouille, *La Geste de Robert Guiscard*, ed. M. Mathieu, Istituto siciliano di studi bizantini e neoellenici, Testi e Monumenti, 4 (Palermo, 1961), II. lines 142–256, esp. lines 235–43.

[5] *The Alexiad of Anna Comnena*, trans. E. R. A. Sewter (Harmondsworth, 1969), I. xi.

[6] William of Apulia, II. lines 129–30.

Map 5 *Southern Italy in the mid-eleventh century*

proprietors. Consequently, when the Norman leaders advanced and settled their followers as vassals on substantial estates, their seignorial institutions had to be adapted to the existing society. Guiscard took over the established state taxes and exercised a loose control over his vassals. His rule in Apulia has been described as 'a legitimation of existing establishments'. While making use of the earlier fortified towns, he built his own castle at Melfi, and most of his followers did likewise in the lands granted to them.[7]

---

[7] J. M. Martin, *La Pouille du VIᵉ au XIIᵉ siècle* (Collection de l'École française de Rome), 277–82; *idem*, 'L'attitude et le rôle des Normands dans l'Italie méridionale byzantine', in *Les Normands en Méditerranée*, ed. P. Bouet et F. Neveux (Caen, 1994), 111–22.

The conquest was much more systematic in Calabria, and was spear headed by the building of castles. Scribla was one of the first; and the more solidly built castle of San Marco Argentano dominated the Norman advance into the Val di Crati. The method was to use the castle as a base from which to force the surrounding region into surrender by systematic ravaging. The next stage was to secure treaties with the towns, take oaths of fidelity, and demand tribute and service. Newly built castles were given to kinsmen and vassals. Feudal institutions were far more of a reality in Calabria than in Apulia. Guiscard's brother Roger was established at Mileto, which was his military base and effective capital until the conquest of Sicily. He brought there as his first wife a Norman from the Grandmesnil family, and founded an abbey peopled with Norman monks. Later, as his power increased, he absorbed far more of the local culture, took over existing institutions, and adopted a more cosmopolitan way of life.

Relations between the brothers were not always harmonious, particularly in 1058, while they tried to exercise a kind of condominium in an ill-defined region south of Squillace. In time they learnt to divide power, with Roger taking charge of the conquest of Sicily. By 1060 he had conquered the eastern part of the island. Though Palermo did not fall until 1072 and the Muslim emirs retained some territories in the south-east until 1091, the Norman conquerors of England were boasting a very few years after 1066 that their fellow Normans had occupied Apulia and conquered Sicily. Roger steadily consolidated his power as count of Calabria and Sicily. Meanwhile Robert Guiscard looked further afield to the Balkans; after capturing the port of Bari in 1071 he began to plan attacks on the Byzantine empire. His ambition can only be conjectured. It was said by Amatus that he aimed at the imperial throne; he certainly wished to secure his Italian lands from any possible reconquest by the Greeks, and was prepared to support an imperial contender. Attack was his surest form of defence, and conquest in the Balkans would protect his shores from raids or invasions by imperial armies.

The assault on Durazzo in 1082–3 would have been impossible if the Normans had not begun to build up a fleet of their own and equip it for combined naval and military operations.[8] It was many years after the arrival of Norman troops of cavalry in southern Italy before

[8]   D. P. Waley, 'Combined operations in Sicily, AD 1060–78', *Papers of the British School at Rome*, 22 (1954), 185–205; M. Bennett, 'Norman naval activity in the Mediterranean c. 1060–c.1108', *ANS*, 15 (1993), 41–58.

(in the words of D. P. Waley) 'the Vikings found their sea-legs again'. This, however, is something of a picturesque exaggeration. What the Normans learnt in the Mediterranean was not to do as the Vikings had done, namely transport their warriors by sea and capture horses in the lands they invaded; they learnt the art of horse-transport and so carried together the men and horses they had trained in the complicated manoeuvres of mounted warfare. Normans, no longer Northmen, they were fighters on land; they relied throughout on the naval skills of the native populations in their combined operations.

At first the Normans used the ships already plying in the Mediterranean, either fishing boats or trading ships, which may have included light transports; after the capture of Bari some larger galleys appear. The mariners, variously described as 'Greeks', 'Calabrians', 'Apulians' or 'men of Bari' appear to have been Byzantine subjects. This was in keeping with the Norman practice of taking into their employment any local troops willing to serve for pay. The Byzantines appear to have been capable of transporting some horses, a skill possibly inherited from the late Roman world. Horses were certainly transported across the straits of Messina for the first assaults on Sicily. Otherwise local ships were used principally to help in investing or capturing ports. They were essential in the successful sieges of Bari in 1071 and Palermo in 1072. After 1076 chroniclers began to refer to construction of ships by the Normans. With the building of larger transports the Norman fleets began to learn new and effective tactics. By 1107 Bohemond's fleet was strong enough to persuade a Byzantine fleet to refuse battle. While Greek fleets, especially when allied with the Venetians, remained formidable, there is some truth in the claim that 'there was a momentum of conquest about the Franks in the Mediterranean, rather like that of an invading tribe. Once this became centrally directed it was all but unstoppable.'

The first attacks in the Balkans never achieved more than temporary success, and within a decade the eastward drive of the Normans was caught up and submerged in the crusading movement. Of more lasting importance was the consolidation of power in southern Italy and Sicily, which continued hesitantly against a background of disputed successions, minority rule, and frequent rebellions. By the beginning of the twelfth century the two most formidable rulers had died, Robert Guiscard in 1085 and Count Roger of Sicily in January 1102. The death of Guiscard occurred when he had left Bohemond, his son by his repudiated wife Alberada, to continue the Balkan campaign from Durazzo. Whether or not he intended Bohemond to have any share

Table 3   The Hauteville rulers in southern Italy (simplified)

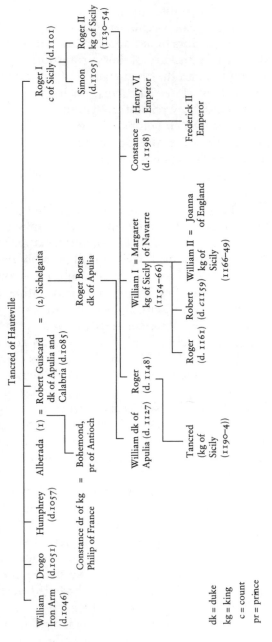

dk = duke
kg = king
c = count
pr = prince

in his southern Italian heritage, his son by his second wife, Roger 'Borsa', aided by his formidable mother the Lombard Sichelgaita, entered unopposed into the whole of it. Bohemond may have been intended to have a Balkan inheritance if it could have been won; but he was driven back by the Byzantines and had to be content with the cities and lands he could induce Roger Borsa to cede to him (including Bari and Taranto), until the First Crusade opened the road to Antioch.

Southern Italy was further disturbed after the death of Count Roger of Sicily was followed by that of his eldest son Simon in 1105. This left his younger son Roger II, a boy of six, as heir, under the guardianship of his mother Adelaide, Roger's third wife. Roger II's inheritance consisted of Calabria and Sicily; the mainland territories of Robert Guiscard were ruled after Roger Borsa's death in 1111 until 1127 by Borsa's son, Duke William of Apulia. During this period, perhaps because there was no Norman ruler of the stature to inspire a new history, the sources consist mainly of brief and patchy annals. Not until Roger II of Sicily acquired the duchy of Apulia after the death of his cousin William did a new historian, Alexander of Telese, attempt a more coherent account of at least the early part of his reign.[9]

---

[9] *Alexandri Telesini abbatis ystoria Rogerii regis Sicilie Calabrie atque Apulie*, ed. Ludovica de Nova, commentary by Dione Clementi, Fonti per la storia d'Italia (Rome, 1991).

6

The Kingdom of Sicily

In any history of the Norman people the kingdom of Sicily, the most cosmopolitan of all their conquests, demands an important place. If the Norman dukes and counts occasionally dreamed of imitating Duke William of Normandy and winning a crown, this was not at first a driving ambition. There was no kingdom in southern Italy for them to take over. Certainly they made the most advantageous marriage alliances open to them. Roger I married two of his daughters to kings, and planned a marriage of the third to king Philip of France. There was a proposal after Roger II came of age in 1112 to marry his mother Adelaide, then aged forty, to king Baldwin I of Jerusalem, and though the validity of the marriage was challenged and it was quickly dissolved, Roger II liked to refer to her as 'queen'.[1] These are hints of aspirations to regal status, but the coronation of Roger II by the papal contender Anacletus II in 1130 resulted rather from a combination of unusual circumstances than from deliberate policy.

When Roger II first came of age he was chiefly interested in the possibility of extending his power in the Mediterranean to make it safe for trade.[2] In 1127 he succeeded in reoccupying Malta, and might have been drawn into a campaign along the Spanish coast had not the death of his cousin William of Apulia renewed his hopes of uniting the Hauteville lands in southern Italy. William left no legitimate heir, and civil disorder broke out as the powerful cities under his rule, particu-

---

[1] Reinhard Elze, 'Zum Königtum Rogers II von Sicilien', in *Festschrift P. E. Schramm zu seinem siebzigsten Geburtstag von Schülen und Freunden zugeeignet*, 2 vols (Wiesbaden, 1964), I. 92–116; L.-R. Ménager, 'L' Institution monarchique dans les états normands d'Italie', in *Cahiers de Civilisation Médiévale*, 2 (1959), 303–31, 445–68.

[2] David Abulafia, 'The Norman Kingdom of Africa and the Norman expeditions to Majorca and the Muslim Mediterranean', *ANS*, 7 (1985), 26–49.

larly Salerno, Troia, Melfi and Venosa, began to go their own way. This was the point when Alexander of Telese, writing only a few years later, saw the hand of God directing Roger of Sicily towards the establishment of a kingdom.[3] Although the need to restore peace was a traditional justification for the seizure of power by a successful claimant, it was all the more persuasive since Roger was a lawful heir of Hauteville stock as well as an ultimately successful military leader who won the blessing of the Church. He was near to Malta when the news of his brother's death reached him, and he acted promptly by sailing to Salerno and negotiating the surrender of the duchy and of Amalfi. Three years of fighting were necessary to overcome rivals in southern Italy and win the grudging recognition of Pope Honorius II. Relations with the Church were complicated when the death of Honorius in February 1130 was followed by a divided election. One of the rival popes, Innocent II, secured widespread support in France and elsewhere north of the Alps, but Anacletus II was established in Rome. It was he who, needing powerful military support, finally crowned Roger as king of a new Sicilian kingdom with its capital in Palermo.

The exact circumstances are obscured by the dubious authenticity of surviving texts of Anacletus's bull. While Roger welcomed the formal approval of a pope for his status, his own views are perhaps best expressed in a famous mosaic in Palermo. There in the church of St Mary of the Admiral (the Martorana), founded by the admiral George of Antioch, a mosaic dating from between 1146 and 1151 shows Roger receiving the crown from Christ himself.[4] Alexander of Telese recorded an unsubstantiated tradition that in ancient times a kingdom had existed in Sicily with Palermo as its capital.[5] The legend was a convenient justification for the more realistic claim that rule over Sicily, Calabria, Apulia and other territories extending almost to Rome was sufficient to justify royal rather than merely ducal status. Palermo, the capital of Count Roger I, was Roger II's natural choice as the centre of his dominion.[6]

Roger's position was reinforced after the schism ended; Innocent II, under duress, reluctantly agreed at Mignano to invest him with the kingdom of Sicily. Roger in return swore fidelity, and a papal bull confirmed his status as king of Sicily, with the duchy of Apulia and the

---

[3] Alexander of Telese, II. 1 (p. 23).
[4] Ernst Kitzinger, 'The mosaics of St Mary's of the Admiral in Palermo', *Dumbarton Oaks Studies*, 27 (Washington, 1992), plate XXIII. See plate 17 below.
[5] Alexander of Telese, II. 1 (p. 23).
[6] Donald Matthew, *The Norman Kingdom of Sicily* (Cambridge, 1992).

principality of Capua. It repeated incidentally the tradition that in ancient times Sicily had been a kingdom. This did not put an end to friction with successive popes, particularly over royal rights to churches; disputes continued until in 1156 Adrian IV reached a settlement with Roger II's son king William at Benevento. By this treaty William agreed to perform homage and swear fidelity; the limits of his kingdom were guaranteed, and he secured confirmation of extensive freedom from papal control for the Sicilian Church.

Politically the kingdom tentatively established in 1130 had been secure from the time of Innocent's first submission. From 1140 Roger II became more and more active in introducing administrative and financial measures that affected the whole territory under his control. Though the second Norman kingdom was brought into existence much more slowly than the first, and was very different in its constituent elements, its development became more capable of comparison both with Norman England and with other European kingdoms. At the same time changes in society and government began which brought to an end the kind of world in which the Normans had made so remarkable an impact.

The Normans won power in southern Italy through their military strength and their ability to enforce law. They acquired nobility by appropriating wealthy estates and intermarrying with the local aristocracy. Family connections remained important throughout the whole period of Norman rule. Once the Hauteville had established their authority they quickly spread a network of kinship across the duchies. Norman families such as the Grandmesnil and later the Bohun and Lacy were prominent. The sons of William of Moulins-la-Marche fled to Italy after the treachery and forfeiture of their father and settled there.[7] Ties of homage and fidelity bound them to the Hauteville; marriage ties increased the nobility and prestige of new families, such as those of Montescaglioso and Conversano.[8] By the middle of the twelfth century royal marriage alliances had become instruments of royal policy, culminating in the marriage in 1177 of King William II to Henry II's daughter Joanna, and of Roger II's daughter Constance to Frederick Barbarossa's son Henry, the future

[7]   G. A. Loud, 'How "Norman" was the Norman conquest of southern Italy?', *Nottingham Medieval Studies*, 25 (1981), 13–34; L.-R. Ménager, 'Pesanteur et étiologie de la colonisation normande de l'Italie', in *idem, Hommes et institutions de l'Italie normande* (Variorum, London, 1981), IV.
[8]   Vincenzo D'Alessandro, 'Nobiltà e parentela nell' Italia normanna', *ANS*, 15 (1993), 91–7.

emperor. But until the Sicilian inheritance was caught up in the imperial ambitions of Constance's son, Frederick II, the Hauteville power and influence preserved the Norman traditions of the kingdom, even while the Norman customs of the age of settlement were becoming merged in the varied customs of a multi-cultural region.

As in Normandy and England, good relations with the Church were an essential part of acculturation. Since the ecclesiastical organization of southern Italy was very nearly as complicated as the political, this was a difficult task. Bishoprics were small and numerous, and in the provinces where Byzantine rule still lingered the church was Greek. Moreover the boundaries of ecclesiastical provinces cut across political boundaries. Some of the great abbeys, notably La Cava, were Lombard foundations. St Benedict's great abbey of Monte Cassino, the cradle of the Benedictine order, was recovering from a period of trouble and disorder; under Abbot Desiderius, elected in 1058, it was closely allied to the reforming papacy. Because of the proximity of the papal states, relations with the papacy had a political side that had not troubled the Normans in their homeland. By offering military protection to popes in times of schism and invasion by imperial armies, the Norman princes were able to extort concessions of privileges from their reluctant protégés. Yet however uneasy the relationship became from time to time, the Norman rulers needed papal approval for reorganization of the Church and for the creation of new bishoprics. Their vassals were as anxious as they were to be on good terms with their local monasteries, whether Orthodox Greek or Latin, and though depredations occurred from time to time and were denounced as barbarous in some monastic chronicles, many abbeys and secular lords co-existed harmoniously. The Lombard abbey of St Sophia in the papal enclave of Benevento received much of its wealth from Normans settled in the neighbouring principality of Capua.[9]

The Hauteville themselves aimed at toleration. They did not attempt a 'Normanization' of the Church; the replacement of Greek by Latin prelates was a gradual process, and initially they gave generously to Greek monasteries including La Cava. But they had a natural preference for the familiar rites of the great Benedictine houses of their homeland, and this, combined with the influence of Monte Cassino, probably accounted for the continued endowment of Benedictine abbeys after the newer orders were gaining ground in Northern Eur-

[9] G. A. Loud, 'A Lombard abbey in a Norman world: St Sophia, Benevento, 1050–1200', *ANS*, 19 (1997), 273–306.

ope. Robert Guiscard and his kinsfolk established Norman monks in Benedictine houses close to their principal castles. Robert Guiscard welcomed a group of exiled monks from Saint-Évroult with their abbot, Robert of Grandmesnil, and gave them extensive estates with the church of Sant' Eufemia in the valley of Nicastro. The impressive extent of the ruins of the abbey, though now overgrown with ivy and almost hidden by bamboo, bear witness to its former greatness. Shortly afterwards Guiscard established Benedictine monks in a former Lombard abbey at Venosa, destined to become the mausoleum of the Hauteville dukes of Apulia.[10] A second colony from Sant' Eufemia was established in the abbey of La Trinité at Mileto, under the patronage of Count Roger, whose principal Calabrian castle was there. After the conquest of Sicily he carried monks with their familiar liturgies to Catania and Palermo.

Castles played their usual part in conquest and settlement. Constant enlargement and rebuilding has left little of the work of the earliest Normans visible. Some mottes appeared in Sicily as well as in Calabria; often the site was changed once a settlement had become permanent. In parts of Sicily the absence of trees meant that wooden structures, which played so important a part in the early motte and bailey castles of Normandy and England, could not be constructed. Instead in places like Sperlinga near Nicosia advantage was taken of spurs of stone, where precipitous slopes could be shaped artifically so as to lodge buildings at two levels.[11] Earlier Greek or Muslim fortifications were adapted for coastal defences. The great castles that the Norman aristocracy used as their homes, administrative centres, and springboards for further conquests adopted new techniques of fortification as these were developed in Byzantium and Palestine, as well as in France and Normandy.

Contingents of trained and mounted knights remained at the heart of the available military forces. Besides these the traditional duty to help in defence, which had existed since a very early date, could be called upon to provide foot soldiers and lightly armed horsemen, as well as money and labour services to construct and repair fortifications and bridges. One of the major administrative tasks undertaken by the first Norman kings was to record the military potential of their kingdom. Of the various inquests made between 1150 and 1158 the

---

[10]   Hubert Houben, 'Roberto II Guiscardo e il monachesimo', *Benedictina*, 32 (1985), 495–520.
[11]   A. J. Taylor, 'Three early castle sites in Sicily: Motta Canastra, Sperlinga and Petralia Soprana', *Château Gaillard*, VII (Caen, 1975), 209–14.

most detailed and comprehensive is partially recorded in the so-called *Catalogus Baronum*.[12] As its editor, E. M. Jamison, points out, this has often been believed mistakenly to be a feudal register, whereas its purpose was to record the notable levy during those years of the *magna expeditio* (roughly equivalent to the *arrière-ban* in France) summoned in times of great danger by the king from the duchy of Apulia and the principality of Capua. The general obligation of every free man to serve 'became adjusted to the material needs available for supplying its cost'. It fell on allodial properties and churches exempt from normal military service as well as on feudal tenants, who already owed ordinary military service for their fiefs. Such tenants figure prominently in the *Catalogus*, but the record is of their wider obligations in times of emergency and the feudal details are incidental. It is not an exact parallel with the *cartae baronum* of 1166 in England. Roger was, however, active in organizing the feudal service; he created, probably in 1142, a new category of military fiefs owing service to the king.

Roger II's measures for the assessment of the resources of his kingdom, the improvement of trade and the provision of effective justice occupied him throughout his reign from 1140 onwards. He was responsible for updating the details of landholding, for reforming the coinage, and for issuing a series of royal edicts which (though they may have been issued piecemeal) certainly led to the greater uniformity of legal measures recorded in the later *Assizes* of the kingdom. The earliest land surveys taken in the island of Sicily date from before Roger's reign there began in 1105. They were kept in the *diwan* (in Latin the *duana de secretis*) and listed the boundaries of estates, the details of their values and the names of serfs attached to the land; they were valuable evidence enabling royal officials to settle disputes about ownership. As the information depended on oral testimony and many of the villagers were Muslim or Greek, Arabic and Greek were the common languages of record. Changing boundaries as well as changes in land ownership made periodic revision desirable to bring them up to date. The 1140s were a time of considerable boundary revision, and the organization of the central *diwan* became more clearly defined, particularly during the years when the admiral George of Antioch was

[12] *Catalogus Baronum*, ed. Evelyn Jamison, Fonti per la storia d'Italia, no. 101 (Rome, 1972); *idem*, 'Additional work on the *Catalogus Baronum*', *Studies on the History of Medieval Sicily and South Italy*, ed. Dione Clementi and Theo Kölzer (Aalen, 1992), 523–85, at 525–9.

active in the royal administration.[13] At first records were kept in Arabic with some translation into Greek. Latin first appeared when officials from the educated citizen class of Bari and Salerno and Capua began to be employed in Palermo. It became permanent after the chancellor, Maio of Bari, was given greater authority during the last two years of King Roger's life and the minority of his son William I. Maio's rise meant that 'the typically Greek office of great admiral was captured by the Latin chancery'.[14] Under his influence subordinate appointments went, not to the old Greek official families, but to his Italian relatives. Latin began to appear in the records, although it did not become the dominant language in the administration for another quarter century. The activities of the *diwan* were chiefly confined to the island of Sicily until about 1174, when the great admiral Eugenius became involved in fiscal business and the settlement of boundary disputes in Salerno; a few years later his activities extended to the city of Amalfi, the duchy of Apulia, and the Terra di Lavoro.[15]

Increasing specialization in the *diwan* was matched by similar changes in the judicial side of the *curia regis* under both Roger II and William I. Between 1143 and 1155 three master justiciars, distinct from the local justiciars, appear. Whereas the duties of earlier members of the *curia* had been political, executive and advisory, theirs were purely judicial. At first litigants from all the provinces were judged in Palermo; only after about 1175 did it become normal for master justiciars and constables to take the final decisions in cases arising in the two mainland provinces.[16] All this was in many ways comparable to changes taking place in other western European kingdoms, notably in England. It was a stage in the formation of states in which power was becoming increasingly centralized, but without stifling local institutions rooted in custom.

A further attempt at organization in Sicily was undertaken by Roger II when he introduced a major change in the currency in 1140. He did not, however, attempt to centralize the coinage, and that of the mainland provinces remained distinct. The currency was not corrupt, but it was complicated and there were complications in design due to the different religions and cultural traditions of the island's inhabitants[17]

---

[13] Matthew, *Kingdom of Sicily*, 219–28.
[14] Evelyn Jamison, *Admiral Eugenius of Sicily: His Life and Work* (London, 1957), 43.
[15] Ibid., 69–71.
[16] Evelyn Jamison, 'Judex Tarantinus', in Jamison, *Studies*, 467–522.
[17] Philip Grierson, 'The coinages of Norman Apulia and Sicily in their international setting', *ANS*, 15 (1993), 117–32.

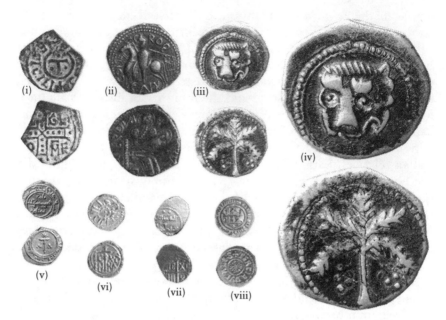

Plate 15   *Norman coinages of Apulia and Sicily, slightly reduced in size. By kind permission of Philip Grierson.*

  (i)   Follaro of Roger I (1072–1101); 3.81g.
 (ii)   Follaro of Roger I (showing Virgin and child on one side and a mounted knight on the other); 10.36g.
(iii)   Restored copper follaro of William II (with lion's mask inspired by a classical coin of Messana and a palm tree copied from ones of Palermo); 10.39g.
(iv)   The same coin enlarged.
 (v)   Sicilian tari of Roger I (1072–1101) or Roger II as count (1105–30); 1.01g.
(vi)   Sicilian tari of Roger II, struck after 1140; 1.34g.
(vii)   Sicilian tari of Roger II c.1130; 0.90g.
(viii)   One-third ducalis of Roger II (with Arabic dating) AH538 = AD1143/4; 0.75G.

(plate 15). The Lombard provinces in southern Italy had, like the Greek provinces, made considerable use of Byzantine coinage reformed by Alexius I Comnenus in 1092, though there were mints which struck coin in the smaller duchies of Gaeta, Sorrento, Capua, Amalfi and elsewhere. Salerno was the principal mint of the duchy of Apulia. In Sicily the Normans took over the former Arab mints at Palermo and struck coins in both gold and silver; they established a mint at Messina, staffed by Arab workmen. The changes were described by Philip Grierson as 'a process of gradual adaptation'. The dies had to be changed to eliminate the Muslim declaration of faith, which was replaced by the Greek letter *tau*, sometimes used for a cross in art. After 1130, when Roger became king, a cross replaced the *tau*.[18] The thematic contents remained varied, being partly Byzantine with figures of the king and some saint, or Muslim with a Cufic inscription; occasional variations occur, such as the purely western image on one coin with a Virgin and Child on one face, and a mounted knight with lance and banner on the other. The chief changes of substance after 1140 were in the weights of copper and gold coins, and the use of alloys with varying copper and silver content. Although the coinages of southern Italy never had the stability of the English coinage they show the merging of a great variety of cultural influences.

The reigns of Roger II and William I provide the high point of Norman influence in the kingdom. The heirs of the Hauteville still held the highest authority in a kingdom that was wealthy and, in spite of cultural diversity and active regional government, still centralized in the king's court and palace in Palermo. Some of its characteristics, particularly the military strength, the kinship network, the ability (in spite of intermittent friction) to influence and use the Church, were still perceptibly Norman. But it had taken on some royal trappings from Byzantium and Egypt. An administration had developed with powerful (if jealous and sometimes seditious) chief officers who were capable of taking over the government when the king was ailing or a minor. The authority exercised by the admiral Maio of Bari during the declining years of King Roger would not have been possible even thirty years earlier. Gradually the history of the kingdom of Sicily ceased to be directly involved with the history of the Norman people, and by the end of the twelfth century, when the royal dignity had been inherited through the female line by the boy who was to become Emperor Frederick II, Sicily was caught up in imperial history. Whatever the later misfortunes of the kingdom it was a remarkable witness, even after it had ceased to be Norman, to the state-building propensities of the Normans.

[18] Ibid., 123; Lucia Travaini, 'Le prime monete argentie dei Normanni in Sicilia', *Rivista italiano di numismatica*, 92 (1990), 171–98.

7

Mediterranean Expansion

Southern Italy provided a launch-pad for further expansion in the Mediterranean region. Advance was limited by the Byzantine Empire and by the various Muslim powers established in the Near East, North Africa, Spain and the Balearic islands. The conquest of Sicily had completed their expulsion from Italy; it was less easy for the Normans to win a foothold in Africa or do more than hold back any further advances in Spain. However, a new opportunity was offered in the eastern Mediterranean when new invaders from Asia, the Seljuk Turks, overran Asia Minor and inflicted a disastrous defeat on the

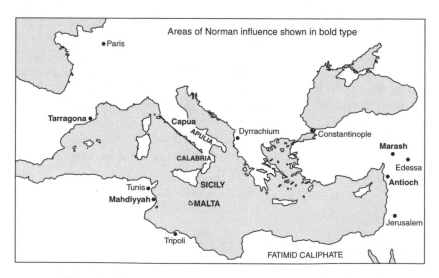

Map 6   *The Mediterranean showing Norman conquests*

Byzantine forces at Manzikert in 1071. The need for reinforcements immediately attracted more Norman knights to offer their services to the emperor. They provided valuable auxiliaries, always on the lookout for gifts of land to settle their families. For a quarter of a century, however, there was no hope of building lasting lordships, as their ancestors had done in Italy; the opportunity came with the crusading movement.

Before that time the Normans had made a significant addition to the myth of their destiny. After the Turkish victory at Manzikert the city of Myra fell to the invaders. It was widely revered as the burial-place of St Nicholas, whose cult was widespread and popular in both Latin and Greek churches. Italian ships trading to the region often carried pilgrims to visit the shrine. The Norman capture of Bari gave them control of part of the trade, and by 1087 an important group of citizens and sailors was able to forestall the Venetians and carry out a successful raid on Myra. The 'mariners' (as they were called) succeeded in breaking into the tomb of St Nicholas and taking the saint's body from the unwilling but powerless handful of Greek monks who guarded it. From 1087 the feast of the translation was celebrated on 9 May, and two years later the relics were installed in the magnificent church of St Nicholas at Bari.[1] The city, significantly, had been ceded to Bohemond just before the consecration of the basilica. The Normans were likely in any case to have claimed that the translation showed the saint's deliberate choice to leave the place where the Byzantine emperor was unable to give protection, and to seek refuge under the strong arm of the new power arising to dominate the eastern Mediterranean: the Norman power. This picture was appropriate to the ambitions of Bohemond, frustrated after the failure of the Norman invasion of the Balkans in 1081–2. The crusading movement provided his opportunity.[2]

In 1096 a group of Norman crusaders led by Robert Curthose chose to avoid the pilgrim route across Europe and travelled through Italy on their way to Jerusalem. They wintered in Apulia and Calabria. Bohemond, who had been helping Duke Roger Borsa in a general investment of the duchy of Amalfi, at once took the cross and was joined by a large group of ambitious magnates, mostly from Norman families. Among them was his kinsman Tancred (either a nephew or a cousin), his cousin Richard of the Principality of Salerno, and Hermann of Canne, together with other vassals of Roger of Sicily and

[1] Orderic, iv. 54–69.
[2] R. B. Yewdale, *Bohemond I, Prince of Antioch* (Princeton, 1924).

Roger Borsa, including Robert of Sourdeval.[3] Bohemond's experienced planning enabled them to cross safely to Bulgaria. Thence the contingent obtained a safe-conduct to Constantinople. In a tense situation, since the emperor Alexius was suspicious with good reason of the motives of Bohemond, they were enabled to cross the Bosphorus after taking oaths of fealty and performing homage. Tancred and Richard of the Principality, however, succeeded in making the crossing secretly with a group of humbler crusaders, and took no oaths. Their hopes and intentions were clear from the start.

The Norman contingent in the crusading army, which included both men from Normandy and south Italian Normans, took the cross for a variety of reasons. A considerable number, particularly those from Normandy, shared the ambition of their leader Duke Robert Curthose, whose principal aim was to reach Jerusalem and restore the Holy Sepulchre to Christian hands. Robert himself was amongst the many who, their task accomplished, returned home. Others decided to remain in the new Frankish kingdom of Jerusalem. But many Normans from Italy, led by Bohemond, Tancred and Richard of the Principality, were out to establish principalities of their own in the course of fulfilling their vows. They were men already used to living alongside Muslims in Sicily, and either fighting against, or negotiating with, the Byzantine emperor. They had at least some knowledge of the conditions likely to prevail in the former provinces of the empire. While aiming at winning lordships of their own, they were not entirely averse to holding them as fiefs of the empire. However, as friction arose during the long and hazardous journey through Asia Minor and Syria, and particularly at Antioch, where they waited in vain for help to be sent by Alexius, Bohemond at least began to aim at an independent principality. He was one of the most successful military commanders and played an important role during the long delay at Antioch. On the whole the crusaders by passed most of the castles along their route and returned later to capture them; but Antioch with its formidable fortifications and strong garrison blocked the way to further advance and had to be captured. Even after its capture the crusaders were besieged in their turn. Bohemond took a leading part in the great battle fought outside the walls, when the besieged crusaders marched out, confronted, and defeated a strong army of Turks. Reluctant to hand over the city to Alexius, and determined not to allow any hostile

[3] Evelyn Jamison, 'Some notes on the *Anonymi Gesta Francorum* with special reference to the Norman contingent from South Italy and Sicily in the First Crusade', in Jamison, *Studies*, 275–300; Orderic, v. 36 and n. 1.

power to occupy it, Bohemond soon turned back from the main army and took Antioch into his own hands, thereby violating his oath to Alexius. Neither he nor Baldwin de Bouillon, who turned aside to capture Edessa, took any part in the capture of Jerusalem; but both men fulfilled their crusading vows by making a pilgrimage to the Holy Sepulchre in 1099.

The political outcome of the crusade was the establishment of a kingdom of Jerusalem, counties at Edessa under Baldwin de Bouillon and Tripoli under Raymond of Toulouse, and a principality at Antioch under Bohemond. Edessa was short-lived; it fell to the Turks in 1151; of the others Antioch, which finally fell in 1268, survived the longest. This may have been due in part to its strategic position; but some of the strength of this most Norman of all the crusading states may have resulted from its institutions and military organization. The foundation was laid by Bohemond and his nephew Tancred, who were schooled in the traditions of Norman Sicily. From 1100 to 1103, when Bohemond was a captive of the Turks, and from 1105 when he was in Europe recruiting forces for a new crusade, Tancred acted as regent in Antioch; and he ruled it as prince after Bohemond's death in 1111. These two men left a perceptibly Norman inheritance in a principality that was racially and culturally as mixed as Sicily, and was influenced also by the more general Frankish customs prevailing throughout the crusader states.

As in England and southern Italy an aristocracy that was culturally Norman was imposed on a racially mixed population.[4] Unlike the other Franks they had the advantage of familiarity with Orthodox Christians and Muslims; some of them had linguistic skills. Both Tancred and Richard of the Principality spoke Arabic and were able to negotiate with the Turks. Tancred's skills had been shown at Jerusalem; Richard was active and trusted as Bohemond's negotiator and envoy both during the periods of his captivity and when he was present and ruling in Antioch. The Normans brought with them customs of feudal lordship and vassalage, which helped to strengthen the central authority of the prince. Central power, which might have been weakened during Bohemond's long absences from the principality, was preserved in the capable hands of his kinsman Tancred, aided by loyal vassals who were determined to establish small lordships of their own. Saone, one of the massive castles essential for the security of the kingdom, was impressively enlarged by one of Tancred's chief

[4] C. Cahen, *La Syrie du Nord* (Paris, 1940).

vassals; and the same was true of Margat.[5] Where Antioch differed from the western kingdoms was in the permanence of a state of war. It also had to contend, as a result of Bohemond's long-standing hostility to Alexius Comnenus, with the enmity of Byzantium and the pressure of Byzantine armies on its northern frontiers. Alexius never forgave Bohemond for violating his oath of fealty; good relations were not established until 1137, when Raymond, prince of Antioch, agreed to become the vassal of the emperor John Comnenus and hold the principality by hereditary right as a fief of the emperor.[6]

The population of the principality included a large number of Christians, of whom the majority belonged to the separated Jacobite and Armenian churches.[7] Many of them were monophysites; they had broken away from the Orthodox Church because of theological differences. Since the Latin rulers, unlike the Byzantines who had governed them until the time of the Turkish conquests, allowed them complete freedom of worship, they welcomed the new regime. At the time of the crusade the patriarchate of Antioch was held by an Orthodox incumbent, and Bohemond was content at first to leave him in possession. Before long, however, as in Sicily, though Greek clergy remained to minister to existing members of their churches, new senior appointments went to Latin clergy, and Latin bishops were consecrated to revived sees in northern Syria. During the patriarchate of Bernard of Valence from 1100 until 1135, relations between patriarch and prince were good. Bernard, though neither well educated nor initially very experienced, had the qualities needed for his office. A man of great courage, he was prepared to go into battle and encourage the troops, though not to fight – as Geoffrey of Coutances and Odo of Bayeux had sometimes done in times of crisis in England. Loyal and practical, he was also ready to assume secular responsibility during times of regency, particularly during Bohemond's captivity and after 1119, when almost the whole army of the principality was annihilated at Darb Samata, the 'Field of Blood'. Relations with later patriarchs were more apt to be strained, but during the early years of the principality cooperation with the Church, which had been so crucial in the duchy of Normandy and the kingdom of England, was an important element in its strength. There was toleration too for the Muslims, who made up a minority of the indigenous population.

[5] Robin Fedden and John Thomson, *Crusader Castles* (London, 1957).
[6] Orderic, vi. 508 and n. 1, citing Cinnamus and William of Tyre.
[7] Bernard Hamilton, *The Latin Church in the Crusader States: The Secular Church* (London, 1980), ch. 2.

Plate 16   *The castle of Saone. By kind permission of A. F. Kersting.*

Military arrangements were naturally of paramount importance. The Normans took over the Byzantine strongholds, some of which were in a ruinous condition, and reconstructed and enlarged them. As in Sicily, they adapted their rebuilding to the most defensive sites. Saone is of particular interest for the amount of Norman work still visible, whereas many other castles, including the mighty Crac des Chevaliers on the borders of Tripoli, were greatly enlarged after being handed over to the Hospitallers. Saone was sculpted out of a precipitous mountain ridge; on one side a great rock-hewn channel over sixty feet wide separated it from the ridge (plate 16). The walls rise sheer for ninety feet, and the Normans left a needle of solid stone 'like an obelisk' to carry a bridge across the channel.[8] The main work of building was probably carried out about 1120 by the lord of the fief, William son of Robert, who had been Tancred's right-hand man.

Both buildings and records were characteristically Norman. The rebuilt cathedrals, like the castles, adapted older structures and introduced some traditional features, but they also incorporated new elements and made use of local craftsmen with different styles. The administration was centrally controlled, but not uniform. Where the established institutions were strong they were retained. Local influence was most apparent in financial matters, and the indigenous population provided much of the personnel for the financial administration.

The *curia* of the prince had much in common with that of the county of Apulia at that date. It was made up of the leading vassals, churchmen, and great officers of state – seneschal, constable, marshal, chamberlain and butler. As yet there were no distinct areas of specialization. Since decisions taken in the *curia* related to particular cases and there is no evidence of general pronouncements, there was no room for local custom. There was, however, a distinction between the jurisdiction of the barons and that of the burgesses. Bohemond had made friends with Genoese merchants in order to keep his supply-lines open, and they were allowed to settle in the sea- ports. They had their separate courts, though they were not given jurisdiction over crimes.

Antioch was undoubtedly a Norman principality in its inception; it provided too, for some generations, a land where Latin settlers might hope to establish themselves and their families. Among the first generation of settlers Bohemond's cousin, Richard of the Principality, is particularly prominent.[9] After a chequered career in Bohemond's crusade, serving as an envoy when he was a captive of the Danishmend emir and later of the emperor, Richard spent some years as regent of Edessa. In 1108 he settled in a border lordship of his own at Marash. Once established, he was able to provide for his family: his son Roger acted at times as regent in Antioch, and his daughter Maria became the second wife of Count Joscelin I of Edessa. His career suggests that for a time at least Antioch held out opportunities for second or third sons to establish themselves in positions of wealth and authority, to which they could never have aspired at home.

[8]   Fedden and Thomson, pp. 79–81.
[9]   George Beech, 'A Norman-Italian adventurer in the East: Richard of Salerno 1097–1112', *ANS*, 15 (1993), 25–40.

Outlasting Jerusalem, it was the most enduring of the Christian king-doms in the Holy Land. As elsewhere, however, its survival meant that the Norman element was absorbed in a new political and social structure.

The Norman foothold was far more transient elsewhere in the Mediterranean lands. In Spain, during the later eleventh and early twelfth century ambitious Norman lords joined forces with others from France in expeditions to drive back the Saracens and sometimes to establish lordships of their own. They acted much like the independ-ent Norman adventurers who had first sought their fortunes in southern Italy. Ralph of Tosny was typical of the Normans who set out from about the time of the 'proto-crusade' against Barbastro in 1064, took part in various campaigns, and then returned to Nor-mandy.[10] From the time of the conquest of England King William did not encourage his best knights to leave his service, and the main influx of Normans into northern Spain took place after King Alfonso the Battler appealed for aid against the Muslims in 1114, and crusading privileges began to be granted for fighting in this region.[11] Count Rotrou of Perche was a leader in crusading expedi-tions into Spain. As a lord on the southern Norman frontier, married to a natural daughter of King Henry I, Rotrou naturally attracted Norman knights to his armies. Some, of whom the most successful was Robert Bordet, went in search of lands to settle.

Robert Bordet came from Cullei (now Rabodanges), where his family were vassals of the Grandmesnil.[12] Possibly a younger son with no prospect of a share in the family lands, he seized his oppor-tunity in Tarragona. The archiepiscopal see was revived in 1118 and granted to Oldegar, bishop of Barcelona, even though much of the province still had to be reconquered from the Muslims. Oldegar, 'small and emaciated, but remarkable for his learning and piety', helped to enlist French and Norman knights by preaching eloquently at the councils of Toulouse and Reims, and he urgently needed a defender for Tarragona. He welcomed Robert Bordet as 'prince of Tarragona', and in 1129 Robert paid homage to him and received the county as a fief of the Church. Subsequently Robert journeyed to Rome to receive papal backing; thence he travelled to his Norman

[10] Orderic, iii. 124–5.
[11] J. M. Lacarra, *Vida de Alfonso el Batallador* (Saragossa, 1971); Orderic, vi. 394–7.
[12] L. J. McCrank, 'Norman crusaders in the Catalan reconquest: Robert Burdet and the principality of Tarragona 1129–55', *Journal of Medieval History*, 7 (1980), 67–82, repr. in *Medieval Frontier History in New Catalonia* (Variorum Studies Series, 1996), IV.

homeland and recruited a number of Normans to return and help in the defence of Tarragona. During his absence, his wife Sibyl filled the role often required of wives in the crusading principalities by taking charge of the defence of the city. Orderic Vitalis relates that she used to put on a hauberk (perhaps, like the Virtues in some illustrated manuscripts of the *Hortus Deliciarum* with her armour over her long skirt),[13] and, taking a rod in her hand, to patrol the walls and keep the guard alert. Robert's 'principality', more accurately described as a county, survived until his death in the mid-1150s; unfortunately, later archbishops were less friendly than Oldegar, and the counts of Barcelona gradually whittled away his authority. An isolated Norman county could not stand alone; and though Tarragona survived longer than the transient lordship that Roussel of Bailleul had tried to establish in the Armenian theme of the Byzantine empire in 1071,[14] its privileges were eroded, civil war broke out, and Robert's descendants were forced to withdraw to Mallorca in 1171.

Elsewhere in the southern Mediterranean Norman expeditions arose from activities in the Kingdom of Sicily, and the motives behind them were mixed. It was important for the rulers of Sicily to keep the sea routes clear of pirates and to promote profitable trade, including trade in corn from the fertile island to North Africa. The titles they adopted sometimes suggested imperial leanings; but much of their conduct was pragmatic. They took advantage of divisions and conflicts among the Muslim powers, never attempting the impossible. Roger II was the most active and ambitious.[15] In David Abulafia's words, 'Virtually no corner of the Mediterranean from Byzantium, Jerusalem and Antioch to Spain and the Maghrib escaped his attention as a possible source of wealth and honour.' Malta, however, was his only permanent reconquest and even there the Normans did little more than appoint a mostly absentee bishop and allow the inhabitants, who were mainly Muslim, to remain undisturbed. After sending fifteen ships to help Ramón Berenguer III, count of Barcelona, to conduct his campaign against Muslims in the Ebro valley (in which Robert Bordet took part), Roger's attention was turned towards Africa and the Near East.

In 1148 he despatched a fleet under George of Antioch to root out a nest of pirates on the island of Jerba, off the coast of Tunisia. This

---

[13]   J. J. G. Alexander, 'Ideological representation of military combat in Anglo-Norman art', *ANS*, 15 (1993), 1–24, at 5.
[14]   Shepard, 'The uses of the Franks', *ANS*, 15 (1993), 275–305, at 275–6.
[15]   Abulafia, 'Norman kingdom of Africa', 26–49.

opened the way for advance into the mainland, where the local emirs, harassed by civil conflict and suffering from a severe famine, were glad to accept his protection and the food he was able to supply from Sicily. Within a short while he had driven the ruler of Mahdiyyah out of the city and extended his protectorate along the coast from Tripoli to Tunis and beyond. He had good diplomatic and commercial relations with the Fatimid caliphs of Egypt. His rule was benign, but short-lived, and the invasion of the Almohads marked the beginning of retreat from Africa. Roger's conquests crumbled within a few years of his death. Antioch was to remain the only Norman principality in the Mediterranean, other than the kingdom of Sicily, to endure for more than half a century. And by the time that Antioch was lost, Sicily too had, through war and inheritance, been drawn into the Hohen-staufen empire. It never lost the elements of culture and tradition that it had absorbed during the period of Norman ascendancy, but it was no longer a Norman kingdom.

Part IV

Myth and Tradition

8

The Norman Myth

From the time of Dudo the Normans were never without their historians, and the chronicles of their deeds were built on the foundations
that Dudo had laid. William, monk of Jumièges, based his *Deeds of
the Norman Dukes* on the same plan, giving one book to the life and
achievements of each Norman duke. He was, however, selective. The
Normandy in which he lived had already a richer and more varied
cultural tradition than Dudo's Normandy. William knew different
Scandinavian legends, had read other historical works and saints'
lives, and had been educated in a monastic environment. The abbey
of Jumièges, ravaged by the Vikings in the late ninth century, owed its
restoration to William Longsword. By the time the monk William
wrote it had recovered most of its lost estates and received new
ones, rebuilt a library and furnished it with books, and begun to foster
historical work. Writing in the 1060s, he dedicated his chronicle to
William, 'the holy, victorious and orthodox king of the English by
grace of the highest King's authority';[1] and King William's achievements and conquest of England made up his seventh book.

The Scandinavian legends used by William of Jumièges gave a
leading role to a certain Bjorn Ironside, the son of 'King Lothbroc';
Hasting was introduced into the story as Bjorn's tutor. William
omitted many of the passages in Dudo which dwelt on Rollo's pagan
achievements, and introduced material from the archives and traditions of his monastery to reinforce his account of the revival of
monastic life in Normandy. At the same time, he included a full
account of the rebellions crushed by the dukes, and their successful
struggles against neighbouring rulers. His chronicle, which was short,

[1]   *GND* i. 5.

written in a relatively simple style, and true to the image of themselves
that the Normans were beginning to cherish, became the most popular
of all the Norman histories, and was the groundwork on which
some later medieval chroniclers built. It survives, in part at least, in
over forty manuscripts, together with the additions that later redac-
tors introduced into it. These included Orderic Vitalis in the abbey of
Saint-Évroult and Robert of Torigny, monk of Bec and abbot of Mont-
Saint-Michel. Robert inserted many of the early passages from Dudo
that William had suppressed, and composed a whole new book
devoted to the reign of Henry I. Later vernacular writers owed much
to this latest version. Wace, in his *Roman de Rou*, wrote a poetic
history using many independent oral sources;[2] Benoît of Saint-Maur
for the most part simply translated Torigny's chronicle into French
verse, with minor interpolations of other material.[3] Throughout the
Middle Ages the augmented chronicle of William of Jumièges
remained the standard source for the early history of the Normans.
Only after the rediscovery of the *Ecclesiastical History* of Orderic
Vitalis in the late fifteenth century did his much longer, less structured,
more colourful, more comprehensive history of the far-flung achievements of the Norman peoples, which incorporated *chansons de geste*,
monastic traditions, folklore, and much else in a unique record, come
into its own.

The unfinished biography of William the Conqueror, written by his
chaplain, William of Poitiers, in the 1070s was in a different genre,
with classical antecedents. William of Poitiers, who belonged to a
knightly Norman family,[4] had been trained as a knight before deciding
to study in the schools of Poitiers and become a priest. His studies gave
him a knowledge of the works of Caesar, Sallust, Cicero, Vergil and
other classical authors. His knowledge of Caesar was exceptional in
Normandy at that time. He had Caesar's account of his invasions of
Britain so much at his finger tips that he was able to compare the
Roman invasions in detail with Duke William's 1066 campaigns.
Although he claimed to write true history, not to wander in the fields
of fiction as the poets did, the history he wrote was coloured by

[2] *Le Roman de Rou de Wace*, ed. A. J. Holden, 3 vols (Société des anciens textes français,
Paris, 1970–3).
[3] *Chronique des ducs de Normandie, par Benoît*, ed. C. Fahlin, 3 vols (Uppsala, 1951–7).
See E. M. C. van Houts, 'The adaptation of the *Gesta Normannorum Ducum* by Wace and
Benoît', in *History and Family Traditions in England and the Continent 1000–1200* (Variorum Collected Studies Series, Ashgate, 1999), XI.
[4] William of Poitiers, pp. xv–xvii.

rhetoric and panegyric. It was, however, never so exaggerated as to obscure the reality of his hero's achievements. As an account of the military exploits that enabled the duke to consolidate his power in Normandy, to strengthen and even extend its frontiers, and to prepare for the conquest of England, the biography is unrivalled among his contemporaries.

His description of the first stages in the establishment of Norman power in England after the victory at Hastings begins a new phase in the development of the Norman myth. The Conquest brought a relatively small group of Normans and their allies into contact with a much older kingdom with its own customs and institutions. A python may, by stretching its jaws, contrive to swallow a much larger prey; but England was too large for the Norman python. Even as a dominant minority, the Normans could assimilate the English people and their culture only by changing their own nature. Their historians, lawyers and administrators did not always mean the same thing when they spoke of 'the Normans' or 'the Norman people' during the time of change. Likewise the meaning of 'the English' was changed in their writings in the course of a few decades.

William of Poitiers first faced the problem at its simplest: how to describe the elements in Duke William's army. He had no doubt that William was duke of the Normans, and that his own vassals and their men, even if they came from Brittany or Maine or Aquitaine, were Normans as the term had been understood from the time of Dudo of Saint-Quentin. The army that he saw under Duke William was made up of Manceaux, French, Bretons and Aquitanians, and particularly of Normans; but when he described the disposition of forces before the Battle of Hastings he stated much more simply that Breton knights and those who were auxiliaries were on the left. Apparently the distinction he drew was between those who joined the army under their own leaders, and those who (whatever their origin) were directly under the duke's command and specially bound to him.[5] He was writing of men he knew personally, and any generalizations were probably unconscious. There is a subtle change of emphasis once the duke of Normandy had become king of England. Poitiers noted that Normans and Bretons obeyed William readily as a most acceptable lord; and that when William imposed a code of discipline on the soldiers in his army the Normans were not given greater licence than the Bretons or Aquitanians.

---

[5] William of Poitiers, II. 16, 17, 19.

The process originally attributed to Rollo, of making one people out of many races, was already beginning again in a new setting. It was complicated by the fact that, although some of the auxiliaries and their men returned home, content to have gained experience and a certain amount of plunder, others remained, settled, and became William's men. Officially, from an early date, they were covered by a single term: royal writs in England were normally addressed to all men, 'Franci et Angli' (Franks and English). From the king's point of view, 'Franci', whether meaning 'Franks' or 'French', came to include all who were not English. And, although some customs, particularly those of inheritance, continued to vary for peasants, tenants-in-chief very quickly accepted a common custom. The Breton settlement, for example, was considerable;[6] some men who had fought at Hastings remained, and there was a steady influx of others from knightly families until, a hundred years after the Conquest, Bretons held some 5 per cent of the 'baronies' established in England. Yet even counts of Breton origin, such as Count Alan III of Richmond, only very exceptionally distinguished Bretons from 'Franci' in their charters.[7] As custom crystallized they came to abandon any Breton customs of partible inheritance (just as the Normans gradually abandoned their 'parage' customs); they accepted a common custom of primogeniture, favoured by the spread of military tenures among the nobility.[8] When William of Poitiers wrote, these changes were still to come; but assumptions about 'peoples' were bound to be made before long.

About half a century after the Conquest another historian, English born, but of mixed blood, wrote a general history of the English people.[9] In this the Normans, for all his attempts to distinguish them, played a somewhat ambiguous role. Henry, archdeacon of Huntingdon, planned his *Historia Anglorum* very carefully, as a work of art. His Norman father belonged to the Glanvill family, and his mother was English. In his account of the pattern of history, he claimed that God had afflicted the British with five successive plagues, as a punishment for their sins: the Romans, the Picts and Scots, the

[6] F. M. Stenton, *The First Century of English Feudalism*, 2nd edn (Oxford, 1961), 24–6; Gaillou and Jones, 182–4, 190–2.

[7] *Early Yorkshire Charters*, ed. C. T. Clay, vols IV, V, *The Honour of Richmond* (Yorkshire Archaeological Society, Wakefield, 1935–6), iv. nos 16, 17, 18, 19.

[8] Pollock and Maitland, ii. 269; Jean Yver, *Égalité entre héritiers et exclusion des enfants dotés* (Société d'histoire du droit, Paris, 1966), 289 n. 648c.

[9] Henry, Archdeacon of Huntingdon, '*Historia Anglorum*', ed. Diana Greenway (Oxford, OMT, 1996).

Saxons, the Danes and the Normans. The conquering Normans are sometimes described in vitriolic terms: God in his just will chose them to destroy the English people, 'because he had seen that they surpassed all other peoples in their unparalleled savagery'. The destruction, though spectacular, was not as wholesale as this rhetoric might imply. Henry explained, with some historical justification, that 'scarcely a noble of English descent remained in England, but all were reduced to servitude and distress, so that it was shameful even to be called English'.[10] The nobles, indeed, bore the brunt of the attack; many men of lesser rank, however, survived and kept their lands, along with the peasants.

To take such denunciations out of their context would be misleading. Henry recognized that the Normans had not been merely destructive. Of the five plagues, he considered that the Romans (for a time) ruled splendidly by right of conquest. The Picts and Scots were raiders, who withdrew when repulsed. Worst of all were the Danes, who 'never aimed to possess the land, but rather plunder it, desiring not to govern, but rather to destroy everything'. The Saxons and Normans, after the first onslaught, were constructive. The Saxons conquered little by little by warfare; then they 'built on what they had gained, and ... ruled by laws'. 'Likewise the Normans suddenly and quickly subdued the land to themselves, and by the right of the kingdom, granted to the conquered their life, liberty and ancient laws.'[11] He accepted the widely held Norman view of Harold's usurpation, and William's legitimate claim to the throne by right of kinship. All in all, his interpretations are fairly consistent, with the shock and cruelty accompanying the invasion balanced by the constructive governance that followed settlement.

Henry chose to call the book that he wrote, corrected and polished, the 'History of the English'. In this the deeds of the Normans have a limited place, and their relation to the English gradually changes, because the nature of both peoples was changing. Neither he nor any of his contemporaries ever used the term 'Anglo-Norman', coined by modern historians to describe the culture and government resulting from the amalgamation of two peoples with their different customs and institutions. But the 'English' with whom Henry of Huntingdon identified himself were not the same as the 'English' whose sins God punished by destruction at the hands of the Normans. The Normans

---

[10]   Henry of Huntingdon, 14–15, 403.
[11]   Ibid., 272–3.

too had changed, for increasing richness and variety of culture accompanied greater sophistication of government. To some extent the Normans may have been identified with the ruling classes. There is even a possibility that Henry of Huntingdon sometimes expressed a more subtle distinction. The civil wars, which began when Stephen's claim to rule was challenged by his cousin the Empress Matilda, threatened for a time to separate Normandy from England. Even in England the rivals controlled different parts of the country, and factions appeared in Stephen's court. It has been suggested that Henry of Huntingdon may have contrasted those whose principal interests were in England with 'Normans' whose chief estates were across the Channel.[12] The successive revisions of Henry's book stand as evidence of the gradual changes in his outlook. As a result later historians, whether attempting to trace early hints of the 'Norman yoke' on the one hand, or the readiness of the Normans to adopt English history as their own on the other, could find some supporting evidence in Henry's work.

In the course of revising and again revising his book, Henry modified his already ambiguous narrative by reintroducing the Norman myth in its earlier form. This was done in the battle speeches, which he had omitted in his earlier recensions. Orations put into the mouths of leaders on the eve of battles rehearsed Norman triumphs and victories in different parts of the world. The speech attributed to Duke William on the eve of the battle of Hastings was not the brief exhortation that William of Poitiers suggested might have been made; it was a recapitulation of Norman achievements from the time of Hasting and Rollo, culminating most recently in the triumph over the French at Mortemer.[13] Battle oratory reached its peak when Ailred of Rievaulx imagined what might have been said by Walter Espec, to an army of mixed English and Normans, drawn up around a standard adorned with the banners of St Peter of York, St John of Beverley, and St Wilfred of Ripon to face the invading Scots in 1137:

> Why should we despair of victory, when victory has been given to our race, as if in fee, by the Almighty? Did not our ancestors invade a very large part of Gaul with a very small force and erase the very name of Gaul?...How often did they snatch victory, even against great odds,

[12]   John Gillingham, 'Henry of Huntingdon and the twelfth-century revival of the English nation', in *Concepts of National Identity in the Middle Ages*, ed. S. Forde, L. Johnson and A. V. Murray (Leeds, 1995), 75–101, at 89.
[13]   William of Poitiers, II. 15; Henry of Huntingdon, 388–93.

from the men of Maine, Anjou or Aquitaine? As for this island [Britain] which once the most glorious Julius won after a long struggle and great slaughter of his men, our fathers and we ourselves have conquered it in a short time...Who has conquered Apulia, Sicily and Calabria but your Norman?[14]

So the Norman myth was introduced into English history. It trailed a new cloud of legends with it through the work of Geoffrey of Monmouth, whose *History of the Kings of Britain* was seen by Henry of Huntingdon on a visit to Bec-Hellouin, and noticed with admiration in his own *History of the English*. Geoffrey's account of the legendary foundation of the kingdom of Britain by Trojans and its history in the form of Arthurian legends, included a section of the alleged 'prophecies of Merlin'. This described a dream of Vortigern about a battle between a red dragon and a white dragon, which was interpreted to signify a struggle between Britons and Saxons, to be ended only when there should come 'a people dressed in wood and in iron corselets': obviously a deliberate reference to the armoured Normans in their ships.[15] So the Norman myth was grafted on to the British myth, and flourished in its new form among the second and third generation of settlers towards the end of Henry I's reign. These were the people who had readily accepted the semi-authentic accounts of pre-Conquest laws that stressed their continuity under the Norman kings. Such collections were made for the interest of those involved in law courts of any kind. Other people, with more literary and historical interests, soon encouraged the production of vernacular history.

About 1140 Geffrei Gaimar wrote his *Estoire des Engleis* at the request of Ralph fitz Gilbert's wife, Constance.[16] She belonged to a family probably settled in Hampshire; her marriage took her to Lincolnshire, where her husband was a friend of Walter Espec. It was from Walter that Gaimar borrowed a copy of the *History of the Kings of Britain*, which became, with the *Anglo-Saxon Chronicle*, a major source for his own history. There is nothing of Rollo in Gaimar's work; instead it incorporates cherished local legends of Havelock the Dane and Hereward the Wake. Rollo's story still flourished, but it flourished in Normandy for the edification of the Normans firmly

---

[14]   Ailred of Rievaulx, *Relatio de Standardo*, in *Chronicles of the Reigns of Stephen, Henry II and Richard I*, ed. Richard Howlett, 4 vols, iii (RS, London, 1886), 186.
[15]   Henry of Huntingdon, 558–83; Orderic, vi. 384.
[16]   Geffrei Gaimar, *L'Estoire des Engleis* (Anglo-Norman Text Society, 14–16, Oxford, 1960).

rooted there. They encouraged the vernacular histories of Wace and Benoît of Saint-Maur, along with the Arthurian romances based on Geoffrey of Monmouth.

The Norman myth in its purest form was also kept alive by a historian of mixed blood, who was writing in Normandy. This was the monk Orderic Vitalis. Born in 1075 in England, near to Shrewsbury, he was the son of a French priest and an English mother. When he was ten his father sent him to become an oblate monk in the Norman abbey of Saint-Évroult. His book was more comprehensive even than Henry's; he called it *The Ecclesiastical History*, and it began with the birth of Christ. Though he spoke of himself as *angligena*, 'of English stock', his whole adult life was spent in Normandy, among monks many of whom came from noble or knightly Norman families. So he absorbed and admired the culture of the Normans, their written histories, their oral accounts of their exploits in battle, and the songs that enhanced their achievements, together with childhood memories of the shock and cruelty of the first years after the Conquest.[17] His *Ecclesiastical History* included the most complete account of the history of the Norman people at the time of their far-flung conquests, together with a detached view of their limitations and faults. Like the work of Henry of Huntingdon, it gives a new twist to the Norman myth. This is not surprising, since Orderic wrote in very concrete terms of the men he knew and their families; moreover, he wrote at a time of profound change in both government and social structure.

To Orderic, who made some use of the work of Dudo, even though he classed it as panegyric, and was intimately familiar with that of William of Jumièges and William of Poitiers, the origin myth was uncomplicated. He took it over in its entirety, and saw Rollo (baptized from the time of his conquests) as the founder of the duchy. With the reign of William the Conqueror a new phase began. Up to then, the Normans 'had been more occupied in warfare than in reading or writing books'. To Orderic, strong leadership and law were essential.[18] In the invented death-bed speech he attributed to the Conqueror, he wrote, 'If the Normans are disciplined under a just and firm rule they are men of great valour, who press on invincibly in arduous undertakings...Without such rule they tear each other to pieces and destroy themselves. So they need to be restrained by the severe penalties of the law.' Orderic's own experience of the disorderly

[17]   Chibnall, *World of Orderic*.
[18]   Orderic, iv. 82–3; v. 24–7.

rule of Robert Curthose in Normandy underlined this. As monk and churchman, he always kept his mind on moral issues. Not only should the ruled be restrained by law, the rule must be legitimate. It is doubtful if he would ever have accepted, with Henry of Huntingdon, that the Romans ruled by right of conquest. Conquest played a part, but hereditary right was, to him, of supreme importance; other rights were subsidiary. He emphasized the hereditary claim of King William, through the marriage of the Norman, Emma, and King Æthelred. This was reinforced by Henry I's marriage to Edith/Matilda of the line of Cerdic. To these marriages he linked that of Robert Guiscard and the Lombard Sichelgaita to win power in Apulia.[19] William of Apulia had written in similar terms of that marriage: 'The people who had formerly served under compulsion now gave the obedience due to ancestral right.'[20] Orderic may never have read William of Apulia's epic poem, though there was a copy at Mont- Saint-Michel; he could have come to the same conclusion independently in a climate of opinion favourable to hereditary right.

The reverse side of the coin was Orderic's insistence that failure was due to lust for unlawful and oppressive conquest of lands to which one had no right.[21] For this reason, he considered, Bohemond's attack on Durazzo failed. When Raymond of Antioch agreed to hold Antioch as a fief of the Emperor John Comnenus in 1137, Orderic acknowledged that Bohemond had originally held it unlawfully, and that right was restored by Raymond's submission.[22] But in the kaleidoscope of events he was describing, many details would not fit into a tidy pattern. However legitimate he found the Norman rule in England, he felt that Gilbert of Auffay was justified in rejecting an offer of lands there, 'because he, who lawfully enjoyed a modest inheritance [in Normandy] declined to have any part in plunder'.[23] Boyhood memories of conditions in England, when starving beggars from the devastated lands in Yorkshire found their way as far as the marches of Wales, must have left an indelible picture of the cruelties of conquest. He believed that the Normans were descended from the 'Dani', the earliest invaders of Neustria, who 'were from the first a cruel and warlike people'.[24] He was not, however, indiscriminate in his assess-

[19] Ibid., vi. 168–9.
[20] William of Apulia, II. lines 436–8.
[21] Orderic, vi. 100–3.
[22] Ibid., vi. 508–9.
[23] Ibid., iii. 254–7; cf. iv. 226–7.
[24] Ibid., v. 24–5.

ment of oppression. In spite of his unqualified condemnation of king William's harrying of the North of England, he was careful not to deny the legitimacy of William's rule in the kingdom he had won, even though the English 'were oppressed by the Norman yoke'.[25]

Writing of the Normans in Italy he was less constrained. He could understand the distrust of Alexius Comnenus for 'the perfidious Norman people', whose custom was not to restore rule to their allies, but to take it from them and 'force into utter subjection those whom they ought to liberate and help to recover their lawful authority'.[26] This, indeed, described the method by which Robert Guiscard had established himself in Apulia: a method which, as Malaterra makes clear, Guiscard was not ashamed to acknowledge. Even in writing of Maine Orderic avoided saying that the Norman rule was legitimate in 1060; he explained that the Manceaux rebelled against the Normans and appealed to Azzo, marquis of Liguria (who had married the sister of Hugh IV of Maine), to regain his heritage, 'not for any love of the Ligurians, but so that they could have any reasonable pretext to shake off the yoke of the Normans'.[27]

For Orderic, tradition and previous history established the characteristics of the Norman people when they were building the duchy of Normandy and conquering England. The same tradition influenced the historians in southern Italy, William of Apulia and Geoffrey of Malaterra, when they praised the conquests of Robert Guiscard and Roger, count of Sicily. Even though Orderic's knowledge of their works was second-hand, he trod at first in the same paths. But he was more familiar with the stories of individual men, kinsmen of the founders and monks of Saint-Évroult, who had visited Italy, and whom he knew personally. The experiences they recalled were often coloured by epic descriptions of deeds of prowess. This makes his narrative of Norman expansion in the Mediterranean lands both vivid and one-sided. He showed little knowledge of the various peoples of southern Italy. Whereas he knew that the army of the Conqueror in England had been made up of auxiliaries from different regions as well as the multi-national Normans from the duchy itself, he tends to describe all Guiscard's or Bohemond's followers as Normans, with an occasional side-reference to Lombards. And his emphasis was on the leaders and a certain number of individual lords who never quite

[25] Ibid., ii. 202–3.
[26] Ibid., iv. 14–15.
[27] Ibid., iv. 192–3.

pulled up their roots in Normandy; some of them even returned there. So he exaggerates the influence of Norman monasticism in south Italy; not surprisingly, since Count Roger's favoured abbey founded beside his chief castle at Mileto was first colonized by Norman monks. Later Roger carried some at least of the familiar Norman chants with him to Sicily, and his descendants heard them sung in the Capella Palatina in Palermo. There were similar influences in Spain, where Orderic epitomized the Norman share in the drive against the Muslims in the struggle of Robert Bordet, a knight from the lands of Saint-Évroult, to establish himself in Tarragona aided by his valiant wife Sibyl.[28]

Such an approach was particularly appropriate for the great period of Norman expansion in the late eleventh and early twelfth century. This was an age when, as Thomas Bisson has shown, the stress was on kinship, patrimony and power.[29] Power, exercised by lords, could lead to a presumption of nobility in a time of relatively little government and much force. Yet if law was often circumvented, force had to be justified in custom and morality in order to preserve its gains. Military skill, strong rule, and ruthless enforcement of law characterized the Normans who established themselves and their followers in so many lands. In the later phases of settlement, as they built on the institutions already existing in the lands they had conquered, and intermarried with the native peoples, they became less Norman and more English or Sicilian. Orderic's special emphasis on the Normans in these lands was to be influential much later in the reshaping of the Norman legend. His great work was little known in the Middle Ages; after its rediscovery it became a powerful influence on the story of the Normans in European history, as seen by historians from C. H. Haskins onwards.[30]

The Normans who conquered and settled in southern Italy carried their origin myth with them. The essential elements appear in the works of Geoffrey of Malaterra and William of Apulia, written in the last decade of the eleventh century to celebrate the achievements of the first Norman leaders. Geoffrey of Malaterra, a monk of Norman origin, was thoroughly imbued with the Norman historical tradition, and spent much of his life in the circle of Count Roger of Sicily.[31]

---

[28] Ibid., vi. 402–4.
[29] *Cultures of Power: Lordship, Status and Process in Twelfth-Century Europe*, ed. T. N. Bisson (Philadelphia, 1995), 2, 339.
[30] C. H. Haskins, *The Normans in European History* (Boston and New York, 1915); D. C. Douglas, *The Norman Achievement* (London, 1969).
[31] Gaufredi Malaterra, *De rebus gestis Rogerii Calabriae et Siciliae comitis et Ricardi Guiscardi ducis fratris eius.*

From the ducal monastic foundation of Mileto he moved to Sant'
Agata in Sicily. He wrote at the command of Count Roger himself.
William of Apulia, probably also of Norman stock, had spent many
years in Apulia; his work, dedicated to Urban II and Roger Borsa (the
son of Robert Guiscard by his Lombard wife, Sichelgaita), was
devoted to Guiscard's achievements.

Malaterra may have known the work of Dudo of Saint-Quentin as
well as later Norman chroniclers; to these he added the oral traditions
treasured in the Hauteville family and passed on to him by Roger
himself. All the familiar descriptions of the Norman character and the
Norman people can be found in his pages. He did not attempt to gloss
over the cruelty and cunning of the Normans; but this was balanced by
their resolution in striving for fame and conquest, their military prowess, open-handedness, eloquence and love of justice.[32] Count Roger
himself insisted that the details of his life as a ruthless brigand when he
first came to Italy should be included to show the measure of his
achievement in climbing to great power, wealth and honour. Malaterra also included a suggestion that the Normans were favoured by
God; he described how Count Roger's army, before crossing the straits
of Messina to attack the Saracens in Sicily, offered prayers to God and
his saints for a safe crossing, performed penance, and received com-
munion.[33] At the same time, like William the Conqueror waiting at
Saint-Valery to invade England, he took care that his devotions were
backed by very careful planning. Since the Normans were fighting
infidels, it was easy for him to paint his followers as a people favoured
by the Church: he described how in one battle St George himself,
riding on a splendid white horse and bearing a white banner, advanced
in front of the army.[34]

William of Apulia was less concerned with traditional legends, but
he picked out some of the essential elements in both the original myth
and its later developments.[35] The Norman achievement in Italy no less
than in Normandy was to bring together different races into a single
people. Remembering their early days, he described how they willingly recruited even malefactors, taught them their customs and language, and made one people out of divers races.[36] Then, by marriage
with a noble wife, Guiscard legitimized his conquests, so that the

[32]   Malaterra, I. iii, p. 8.
[33]   Ibid., II. ix, p. 32.
[34]   Ibid., II. xxxiii, p. 44.
[35]   William of Apulia, *Gesta Roberti Wiscardi.*
[36]   William of Apulia, I. lines 165–8.

Lombards who at first had obeyed only under compulsion now gave the obedience due to ancestral right.[37] His poem is an epic, very much occupied with the details of battles on sea and on land. He praised the courage and resourcefulness of the Norman leaders, particularly Guiscard and Bohemond, the son of Guiscard's first marriage to a Norman wife. At the same time, he showed considerable knowledge of Greek affairs, the Lombard background and the affairs of the Papacy, as was to be expected in a work addressed to the half-Lombard Roger Borsa and the pope. The poem ended with the burial of Guiscard beside his older brothers in the family church of Venosa, one of the first Benedictine abbeys to be founded by the Norman leaders. There many of the customs of Norman abbeys such as Saint-Évroult were observed. So the close Norman associations of the Norman leaders were respected at the close of Guiscard's life, though much of his life had been spent in trying to integrate other indigenous peoples and their customs into a single principality under strong rule.

One aspect of the Norman conquests which was to loom large in the Italian sources was their attempted expansion in the Mediterranean. The attacks on Durazzo and other wars against the emperor Alexius Comnenus took William of Apulia's narrative into the Balkans. One slightly earlier, non-Norman source had gone further. In the 1070s Amatus, a monk-historian of Monte Cassino, gave an account of the Normans up to about 1078. Although it survives only imperfectly in a fourteenth-century French poem, which is partly translation and partly paraphrase and comment, it is accepted as authentic.[38] Greatly impressed by the powerful, warlike race of Normans, Amatus describes their deeds, not only in Italy but in Spain, against the Saracens. They appear as Christian champions against the infidel throughout the length and breadth of the Mediterranean world, fighting sometimes in the armies of the Greek emperors. So in Italy a new twist was being given to the myth of the Normans as a chosen people; even before the Crusade launched by Urban II in 1095 they were seen as the spearhead of counter-attacks against the Saracens.

The formation of a Norman state was the most remarkable achievement of the Normans in Southern Italy. It was brought about by the continuing military skill of the Norman leaders, and the powers of assimilation shown in their government. If ability to fight and govern created a new political structure, assimilation produced a new culture,

---

[37] Ibid., II. lines 436–8.
[38] *Storia dei Normanni di Amato di Montecassino*, ed. V. de Bartholomeis (Fonti per la storia d'Italia, Rome, 1935).

and among the changes that took place was a new approach to history.
When serious historical writing began again in the second quarter of
the twelfth century, after a period when the past was recorded in
meagre annals, historians were no longer Normans writing to gratify
a Norman count or duke. Of the two most conspicuous, Falco of
Benevento was a town notary, bitterly hostile to Roger II;[39] Alexander
of Telese was the non-Norman abbot of S. Salvatore, Telese, a monastery in a region ravaged by war, whose main concern was the
maintenance of peace.[40] Alexander regarded Roger as the instrument
of God, divinely ordained to restore order by his conquests. He
himself was neither a Lombard nor a Norman; he belonged to the
indigenous, strongly latinized, population that had existed in the
region since before the barbarian invasions. The history that he
wrote was not an imitation of classical models; it was based on an
older, cultural tradition that had survived several centuries of disrup-
tions.[41] In itself it was an example of a characteristic method of
survival: the offer of a gift or service made by one of the conquered
on submission to a conqueror to secure his protection. So, although
the central theme of the work – that Roger was the instrument of
God's will – also existed as a theme in the Norman myth, the work
itself is not a chronological extension of that myth. Limited in scope, it
does not even follow the lead of Amatus and chronicle Norman
achievements as the triumphs of Christian knights fighting the infidel
in various parts of the Mediterranean. Nevertheless, it provided
material that could be used by later exponents of the myth.

Alexander wrote before Roger's conquest was complete, and so, in
order to uphold his thesis, he sometimes found himself forced to
explain battles that were lost when they should have been won, or
actions that seemed to show Roger as less than merciful and generous.
In 1132, when Roger's advance was temporarily halted by his defeat at
Nocera, Alexander explained that God had punished him for the sin of
pride, in not attributing his previous success to God. Once he had
humbly confessed and made reparation, his triumphs could continue.
After his success had returned, when he captured the rebel fortress of
Montepeloso, he failed to show mercy but punished Tancred of Conversano and other rebels savagely. Some were blinded and others

[39] *Falconis Beneventani Chronicon*, ed. Del Re, Cronisti e scrittori sincroni napoletani
editi e inediti, I (Naples 1845); G. A. Loud, 'The genesis and context of the Chronicle of
Falco of Benevento', *ANS*, 15 (1993), 177–98.
[40] Alexander of Telese, *Ystoria Rogerii regis Sicilie, Calabrie atque Apulie*.
[41] Alexander of Telese (commentary), 177–9, 191–6.

Plate 17 *Mosaic from St Mary's of the Admiral (La Martorana), Palermo,
showing King Roger II crowned by Christ. By kind permission of SCALA.*

imprisoned in chains; their cities were burned. Alexander justified this
cruel treatment of rebels by turning to the Old Testament and finding
an analogy in King Nebuchadnezzar's punishment of Zedekiah for
violating his solemn oath. Zedekiah's sons were killed in front of him,
his own eyes were put out, and Jerusalem was burned.[42] The whole
approach was traditional in its reliance on evidence from the Bible; it
was not specifically Norman. Alexander felt justified in asserting, 'It is
no wonder that he was able with the aid of God to bring all these lands

[42] Alexander of Telese (commentary), 183–4.

under his power, since everywhere he ruled he promulgated such mighty and thorough justice that continuous peace was soon to endure' (plate 17).[43]

The burning of cities, however, was not likely to commend itself to the champions of civic independence, who were already influencing historical writing in Italy. Falco of Benevento's central interest was the history of his native Benevento; he regarded Roger as a tyrant worse than Nero who was stamping out civic freedom. He was prepared to soften his tone a little only after Roger granted a privilege to Benevento. In general, however, he wrote a chronicle very similar in character to the urban chronicles of communal, northern Italy; he was not concerned with the Norman people. The royal power the Normans established in southern Italy subordinated the interests of the cities to their own commercial and political aims. In the flowering of historical writing in the later twelfth century the Norman myth became stifled by a vigorous growth of the types of chronicle such as the *History of the Tyrants of Sicily* of the so-called 'Hugo Falcandus' appropriate to different political structures.[44]

Norman historians presented the Norman people as they seemed to themselves in narratives that combined origin myths with genuine, and sometimes very frank, records of the characteristics revealed in their history. Writers with different loyalties presented a number of different and usually unflattering pictures. Some of these can be found in the writings of Byzantine historians, who had encountered or heard of the Normans in the early Balkan wars and the crusading armies. Others appear in literary works produced in France; the latest in the largest and most varied group of all, modern historians, lawyers and novelists, who have been actively creating a kind of Norman anti-myth up to the present day.

Among the Greek historians the earliest and most balanced was Anna Comnena, the daughter of Alexius Comnenus, who recorded the deeds of her admired father in the *Alexiad*.[45] She had met some Normans, and Bohemond in particular had impressed himself on her memory. Although she used the term 'Norman' only about five times, and usually referred to them together with all the Frankish crusaders as 'Celts', her references, particularly when concerned with the deeds of Robert Guiscard and Bohemond, certainly refer to

---

[43] Alexander of Telese, I. 21.
[44] *The History of the Tyrants of Sicily by Hugo Falcandus 1154–69*, ed. and trans. T. Wiedemann and G. A. Loud (Manchester, 1998).
[45] *The Alexiad of Anna Comnena*, trans. E. R. A. Sewter (Harmondsworth, 1978).

Normans. The picture was not all black; she praised their courage, the intelligence of their leaders, the force of their initial attack, and their naval discipline. They were formidable fighters. The deceit and guile that she condemned were qualities that the Normans themselves recognized, and that some of the earliest leaders, notably Robert Guiscard, even acknowledged with some pride. But Anna became increasingly bitter as she described the deteriorating relations between the Greeks and the Normans. They were barbarians, perjurers, ungrateful, haughty, violent men, money-grubbers, quite immoderate; they surpassed all others in loquacity.[46] The Greek princess attributed their boundless ambition to their humble origins.

Deteriorating relations became more and more apparent in the attacks of later historians, to whom they were barbarians.[47] John Zonaras, John Cinnamus and Eustace of Thessalonica had no words of praise for these enemies and barbarians, with their huge armies. Although the term 'Normans' was never used, Normans were frequently intended in the descriptions of war and ravaging, even when the authors had no first-hand knowledge of the events. They had become stereotyped as ruthless and cruel enemies.

Similarly contrasting stereotypes occur in the vernacular *chansons*, which preserved the traditions of the Normans and their enemies. For the Normans everywhere, in the duchy of their origin, in their southern Italian conquests, and in their crusading lands, the *chansons* recounted and enhanced the achievements of their heroes from the eleventh to the thirteenth century. It was claimed that the *Chanson de Roland* was sung at the battle of Hastings. The setting was nominally the Carolingian realm, but jongleurs superimposed on it the contemporary France that they knew. Conventionally the duke of Normandy who appeared in many of the songs was called Richard, even though Robert I had some claim to be a subject of *chansons* through his pilgrimage to Jerusalem.[48] The eponymous Richard, sometimes identified with Duke Richard I, appears in different settings. He is the founder of Fécamp in *Gormond*, and is praised by Charlemagne in *Aimeri de Narbonne*. In France, however, particularly during the time of intense Norman and French rivalry in the mid-twelfth century, his memory is denigrated. In the *Couronnement de Louis*, dating

[46] *Alexiad*, XII. 9; XIV. 4.
[47] Michel Balard, 'Les Normands vus par les chroniqueurs byzantins du XIIe siècle, in *Les Normands en Méditerranée*', ed. Pierre Bouet et François Neveux (Caen, 1994), 225–34.
[48] René Louis, 'Les ducs de Normandie dans les chansons de geste', *Byzantion*, 28 (1958), 391–419.

probably from between 1131 and 1150, he is seen at his worst. The theme of the poem, one of the cycle of Guillaume d'Orange,[49] is the success of Count William, as the loyal and indefatigable vassal of a weak young king, in preserving a strong, united kingdom with a hereditary crown. Richard of Normandy acts the part of the treacherous, rebellious vassal who repeatedly tries and fails to thwart William. He is first forcibly tonsured and banished to a monastery; after escaping and making a last attempt to ambush William in the forest of Lyons, he is condemned to end his days in prison. So to the French the Norman dukes were cunning traitors, out to disrupt the unity of the kingdom; while in Normandy the tombs of the first two Richards were venerated at Fécamp.

Most persistent of all the anti-Norman myths was the romantic identification of the English with the defeated Saxons and the Normans with the ruling class. The elements of truth in this were soon submerged in the social, linguistic and legal changes of the later Middle Ages, and transformed out of all recognition, first in the constitutional and social struggles of the seventeenth century, and then in the romantic novels and nationalist movements of the nineteenth.[50] The myth of the 'Norman yoke', however, can hardly be said to belong to the history of the Norman people. The Normans of *Ivanhoe* had as little to do with the duchy of Normandy as had the heroic and largely imaginary Vikings popularized by American writers, when 'picturesque' medieval history flourished in mid-nineteenth-century America.[51] Both were quirks of historiography, which could have flourished only after the true Norman people had become confined to the duchy of Normandy where their history had begun. Behind the romantic legends, however, which at least had the virtue of stimulating interest, serious archaeological and historical studies were at work from the early years of the nineteenth century on the realities of the Norman achievement.

[49] Jean Frappier, *Les Chansons de geste du cycle de Guillaume d'Orange*, 3 vols (Paris, 1955–83); *Le Couronnement de Louis. Chanson de geste du XIIᵉ siècle*, ed. Ernest Langlois (Les classiques français au Moyen Age, Paris, 1920).
[50] Asa Briggs, *Saxons, Normans and Victorians* (St Leonards-on-Sea, 1966); M. Chibnall, *The Debate on the Norman Conquest* (Manchester, 1999), 53–5.
[51] Robin Fleming, 'Picturesque history and the Medieval in nineteenth-century America', *American Historical Review*, 100 (1995), 1061–94.

9

The Norman World

'At the beginning of the twelfth century, probably, it was only from a Norman monastery that one could turn his gaze in ever-widening circles to new lands almost without having to travel.'[1] Peter Classen's comment on the history written by Orderic Vitalis points to one aspect of the Norman world as it had developed for more than a century. The bands of adventurers who, from the early eleventh century, set out as mercenary soldiers in search of lands to settle and conquer, and the pilgrims to Monte Gargano, Jerusalem and Compostela, provided a network of personal contacts across Europe. New principalities in southern Italy, Spain and Antioch; a newly-conquered kingdom in England as a base for further advances, all widened the range of Norman settlements without at first breaking the bonds of family and patronage which helped to spread familiar customs, before they were cross-fertilized by the different customs of other lands. When Geoffrey, bishop of Coutances, was elected to a battered and impoverished Norman bishopric in 1049 it was natural for him to turn to a family from his new diocese, the Hauteville, who had made their fortunes from plunder in southern Italy, for resources to rebuild his cathedral. When Robert of Grandmesnil, abbot of Saint-Évroult, was exiled because of the rebellion of members of his family, he set out with a group of monks to enlist the support of his kinsfolk in Calabria, and established a new abbey at Sant' Eufemia. More than half a century later, Robert Bordet, hard-pressed by Muslims in his lordship of Tarragona, visited his native village on the southern frontier of

[1] Peter Classen, 'Res gestae, universal history, apocalypse: visions of past and future', in Renaissance and Renewal in the Twelfth Century, ed. R. L. Benson and Giles Constable (Cambridge, Mass., 1982), 387–417, at 388.

Normandy to recruit fresh troops. Several generations had to pass
before the ties of kinship and loyalty, which kept alive the traditions of
a Norman people, were broken.

These ties were not the only cause of movement. Pilgrimages to
Jerusalem were becoming swept up in the crusading movement, in
which many non-Normans took part. Collectively the western crusaders were known by various titles, particularly as Franks. The *chansons* inspired by wars against the infidel belonged to the general
cultural heritage of Europe. Rome too, which had been a focus of
pilgrimage since the early Middle Ages, drew more travellers when
papal reform led to increased centralization; even when political dis-
turbances drove popes from Rome they held synods and councils
wherever they found refuge, even as far away as Reims or Clermont.
Benedictine abbeys established networks of dependencies; the customs
of Cluny were readily adopted, even in houses that had no constitutional ties with Cluny. Customs and prayer-unions between abbeys
influenced architecture and liturgy and music no less than the daily
pattern of monastic life. Even in the eleventh century famous monastic
schools drew scholars from far afield; within a hundred years cathedral schools and universities were taking over. French, the *lingua
franca* of the educated world, joined the Latin of the schools to
make movement easy for learned Normans among many others.
When Anselm, archbishop of Canterbury, was driven into exile and
set out for Rome to seek support from the pope, he found many
friends in Italy. If his homeland in Aosta had little to offer him, he
found support from Count Roger of Sicily and a welcome at the court
of Urban II. In addition, when he needed a little peace from the heat
and dust of Rome and Capua, he was offered a refuge by a former
monk of his abbey. John, a Roman, had been drawn to Bec by
Anselm's fame, and had subsequently been made abbot of S. Salvatore
at Telese; it was in the abbey's hill-top village of Sclavia (now Liberi)
that Anselm finished writing *Cur Deus homo*.[2] There was nothing
narrow about the Norman world, which is little more than one way to
approach western European culture in the eleventh and twelfth centuries. Nevertheless, that such an approach is possible is a sign of the
reality of the Norman impact on peoples in different regions, and on
the chroniclers writing about them.

The extent of Norman colonization and settlement was determined
by a mixture of individual enterprise and ducal planning. Up to the

---

[2]   *Eadmeri Historia Novorum in Anglia*, ed. Martin Rule (London, RS, 1884), 96–7.

mid-1060s the knights who left Normandy to seek their fortune, either individually or in small bands under a leader, acted on their own initiative. Some were exiled for rebellion in Normandy; many, from families with more sons than the family patrimony could support, went voluntarily in search of lands where they could settle and establish a family. The situation changed when Duke William needed all possible resources to defend Normandy and embark on his greatest enterprise of winning the English kingdom, though troubles at home might still cause emigration. The crusade too drew knights as pilgrims to Spain and the eastern Mediterranean; new kingdoms and principalities attracted permanent settlers at a time of rapid population growth. But the conditions prevailing in the first half of the eleventh century meant that Norman colonization in Italy was piecemeal. As everywhere, it was military; success depended on skill in fighting. Numbers were small, but the units were highly trained. The men who emigrated came from minor knightly families, equipped and trained for warfare, but dependent on their own prowess to succeed and settle. They were likely to look for wives among the local landed nobility. There was no mass emigration or peasant settlement. Travelling light, they were mobile enough to serve all over southern Italy and even in the imperial armies at Constantinople and in Asia Minor. One mercenary captain, Roussel of Bailleul, aimed at independence and built up a short-lived lordship for himself in Asia Minor before being brought to heel by a Byzantine commander. Though sentenced to be blinded he was too valuable an asset for the sentence to be carried out; released from prison he was soon re-employed as a leader in the imperial armies.[3] Another knight, William of Montreuil, became a leader in the papal armies.[4] At first many looked for employment in the Lombard principalities and in the Greek-led campaigns to drive the Saracens out of Sicily. Once Norman principalities had been set up, the new Norman counts willingly enlisted their kinsmen and compatriots in the armies on which their continued power and prosperity depended. But everywhere – as latter in England – a conquering alien minority was imposed on an ethnically mixed indigenous population.

The northern settlers in Italy were not all from the duchy of Normandy; some Flemings and others from the borders of the duchy were included.[5] It has been calculated, however, that a high proportion came from Normandy; other knights were from regions with similar

3   Shepard, 'Uses of the Franks', 275–6.
4   Orderic, ii, 58–9.
5   Ménager, 'Colonisation normande', 313–63; Loud, 'How "Norman"...?', 3–34.

customs. In the early eleventh century obligations arising from fealty were broadly similar in the different provinces of north-western Europe; they were customary and clearly understood, and had not the rigidity of the more contractual obligations incurred with the practice of granting fiefs (*feodi*). The conquerors and settlers in Italy lived by the sword and accepted the type of military lordship that had made for the success of their first Viking ancestors in Normandy. Because they remained a minority after settlement in a potentially hostile country, these bonds of lordship were strong. The newcomers adapted themselves to the indigenous majorities and took over their instruments of government, while preserving this strong lordship. There was no question of importing any kind of 'feudalism', which is no more than a term invented later to describe a sociological concept. But the feudal obligations resulting from the grant of fiefs enhanced the power of the Norman lords. There are some superficial resemblances between the Norman principalities in different parts of Europe; yet not surprisingly each region developed in a way partly determined by its history before the coming of the Normans. Even when Rollo and his followers first settled in Normandy they made use of local Carolingian instruments of government and never imported the Scandinavian popular assembly, the 'thing'.[6] As conquerors in England they accepted the existing local organization of shire, hundred and wapentake, while reinforcing the strength of the monarchy. There was a similar combination of old and new in their various Italian lordships.

   In Italy the Normans took over much from the Lombard dukes and, particularly in the southern provinces, the Greek rulers. An added element in Sicily came from the Muslims. There were military obligations for general defence; there were also the written records of a bureaucratic government, which provided a relatively efficient basis for assessing taxes. To these must be added the mercantile customs of the thriving cities, particularly those, like Bari, engaged in Mediterranean trade. As a result money was available to hire ships and sailors; and individuals without fiefs could be called upon to serve in times of great danger. But because of the threat of Saracen raids and attacks from neighbouring dukes, the military obligations of holders of fiefs were rarely commuted for cash; they might even be increased, and new demands sometimes provoked vassals to rebel. Orderic Vitalis, who

---

[6] L. Musset, 'Gouvernés et gouvernants dans le monde scandinave et dans le monde normand', *Gouvernés et gouvernants*, 2, Recueils de la Société Jean Bodin, 23 (Brussels, 1968).

knew his Normans, was never tired of saying that the Normans were a turbulent people who, unless they were restrained by a strong hand, tore each other to pieces in internal strife. A leader as strong as Roger II, even before he became king, could impose new burdens and force even his most powerful vassals into exile if they resisted him. This led to a trickle of disappointed vassals back to their patrimonial lands in Normandy, or into the new lands of opportunity opened up by the crusades.

In Italy, as elsewhere where the Normans fought and settled, the characteristics that might be described as Norman were contributed, first by the men themselves, and second by the opportunities they opened up for travel across the whole region. The knights were followed or accompanied by monks from their family monasteries, household officers with their experience, craftsmen with their skills, and scholars and jongleurs with their varied talents. Families were the best preservers of tradition; but intermarriage with noble Lombard heiresses and a readiness to appreciate what the peoples among whom they settled had to offer made for change.

The greatest of all the Norman families to thrive in Italy was that of the Hauteville. They carried on some of the customs of their homeland for a century and a half, while absorbing more and more of the culture of the peoples among whom they were living. From an early date they looked for Benedictine monks to provide the services with which they were familiar. Drogo de Hauteville planned to restore the ancient Lombard abbey at Venosa; after his death his brother Humphrey completed the foundation with a group of Benedictine monks from Monte Cassino.[7] Robert Guiscard, however, took the opportunity offered by the appeal of exiled monks from Saint-Évroult to bring the familiar liturgy and monastic customs of his homeland into his Italian duchy. He responded to the appeal of his fellow-countryman, Abbot Robert of Grandmesnil, by establishing him and his dozen monk-companions in the restored abbey of Sant' Eufemia. From this great abbey in the frontier zone between Apulia and Calabria, a number of monks carried their customs to other restored or newly founded abbeys. By this time there were some twenty monks at Venosa; and, either because they were lax or because their customs were unfamiliar to Robert Guiscard, he asked Berengar, son of Arnoul,

[7] L.-R. Ménager, 'Les fondations monastiques de Robert Guiscard, duc de Pouille et de Calabre', *Quellen und Forschungen aus italienischen Archiven und Bibliotheken*, 39 (1959), 1–116.

one of the original Norman monks, to undertake the restoration of the abbey.[8] It became the principal family monastery and mausoleum of Guiscard and his immediate kinsfolk. The necrology of the abbey, entered in the 'chapter-book', contained the names of many prominent Hautevilles, including Robert Guiscard, his brother Count Roger, his son Roger Borsa and grandson William of Apulia, Roger II, king of Sicily, and his first wife Elvira.[9] Roger II himself, though commemorated at Venosa, was buried in his cathedral church at Palermo.

Possibly Venosa or Sant' Eufemia provided the duke with some of the distinguished scribes who had migrated with the first monks from Normandy. Certain clauses in Sant' Eufemia's charter of foundation echo clauses in the Norman charters of Duke William the Bastard.[10] Likewise at Venosa when Robert Guiscard handed over his charter, he gave with it a little knife, the *cannivectus* or *canivet* sometimes used when deeds of gift were handed over in Normandy. Such similarities did not mean that Guiscard wished to use the monks as instruments of 'benedictinization' in his new dominions; he was a generous donor to Greek abbeys also. And there was no monopoly of scripts; some documents were written in Beneventan script. But the ducal family liked to preserve something of the familiar liturgy and legal customs at the heart of their new domains. And certainly, at Venosa, they established a lasting centre of loyalty to their family. The chronicle of the abbey, compiled probably towards the end of the twelfth century, treated Robert Guiscard almost as a saint. It describes the visions of a monk, who had carelessly fallen asleep on Robert's tomb and was commanded to move three times by a terrible voice. In his third vision, a threatening Duke Robert charged the monks with careless administration of their goods, and in particular with the loss of the little knife, the *canivet*, which he had handed over when making his first gifts. After these visions the monks of Venosa always showed great reverence and bowed their heads when passing the tomb.[11] Their loyalty to the family of their benefactors increased in the late twelfth century, when Swabian replaced Norman domination in southern Italy. It was noticed and punished by Henry VI, who seized some of the abbey's possessions near to Foggia, and placed the abbey itself under the administration of the dean of Monte Cassino.

---

[8] Orderic, ii. 100–2.
[9] H. Houben, *Il 'libro del capitolo' del monastero della Santa Trinità di Venosa (Cod. Casin. 334): una testimonianza del Mezzogiorno normanno* (Galatina, 1988), 67–96.
[10] L.-R. Ménager, *Recueil des actes des Ducs normands d'Italie (1046–1127)*, 38–47.
[11] Houben, 'Roberto il Guiscardo'.

A similar desire to be accompanied by monks from his native Normandy was shown by Guiscard's brother, Count Roger. He built his favourite Calabrian castle at Mileto and, in characteristic Norman fashion, founded a great Benedictine abbey just beside it. The first abbot, William son of Ingran, was one of the monks from Saint-Évroult. It was at Mileto that Count Roger married his first wife Judith, the half-sister of Robert of Grandmesnil. There too, and not at Venosa, he chose to be buried. From Mileto he took monks to Sicily, with the result that the familiar chants were heard at Sant' Agata on the slopes of Mount Etna, and in his Capella Palatina in Palermo.[12]

The monastic customs imported from Normandy were already eclectic when they reached Sant' Eufemia. When Robert of Grandmesnil was serving his noviciate at Saint-Évroult he was sent for a time to Cluny to learn some of the Cluniac customs; Bernfrid, a monk of Cluny, accompanied him on his return to instruct the monks of Saint-Évroult. Abbot Robert also had music for the office of St Evroult, which had been composed by Arnulf, the cantor of Chartres, taught to his monks.[13] The service-books used in Palermo show the influence of churches in Burgundy, Paris, and the region of Chartres as well as Normandy. Nothing, perhaps, was more characteristic of the Norman people than the way in which even the strongest Norman customs preserved in the personal devotions of the leading families, never became fossilized. They were always capable of enrichment by other traditions.

The energies of the Hauteville were concentrated in the Mediterranean lands. Robert Guiscard's eldest son, Bohemond, took the road to Jerusalem leading a contingent including many of his kinsmen and vassals in the First Crusade. His principality of Antioch was to attract knights from other parts of the Norman world. Other kinship networks extended even more widely after the conquest of England opened a new realm for settlement by land-hungry Normans. The Grandmesnil, allied by marriage to the Hauteville, show a different pattern of settlement.[14] The founder of the family became established in Normandy as a member of the middling aristocracy. The original family lands were around Norrey-en-Auge and Grandmesnil, not far from Falaise; and a marriage alliance with the Giroie brought domains

[12] D. Hiley, 'Quanto c'è di normanno nei tropari Siculo-Normanni?', *Rivista italiana di musicologia*, 18 (1981), 3–28.
[13] Orderic, ii. 74–5, 108–9.
[14] Joseph Decaens, 'Le patrimoine des Grandmesnil en Normandie, en Italie et en Angleterre aux XIᵉ et XIIᵉ siècles', in *Les Normands en Méditerranée*, 123–40.

Table 4 The family of Grandmesnil

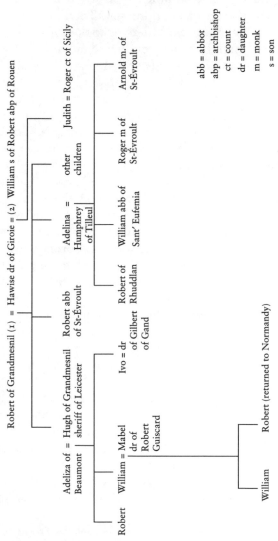

Robert of Grandmesnil (1) = Hawise dr of Giroie = (2) William s of Robert abp of Rouen

Robert

Adeliza of = Hugh of Grandmesnil
Beaumont   sheriff of Leicester

William = Mabel
           dr of
           Robert
           Guiscard

Robert

William   Robert (returned to Normandy)

Ivo = dr
       of Gilbert
       of Gand

Robert abb
of St-Évroult

Robert of
Rhuddlan

Adelina   =
Humphrey
of Tilleul

William abb of
Sant' Eufemia

other
children

Roger m of
St-Évroult

Judith = Roger ct of Sicily

Arnold m. of
St-Évroult

abb = abbot
abp = archbishop
ct = count
dr = daughter
m = monk
s = son

around Echauffour (Orne) and Montreuil-l'Argilé (Eure) to add to their patrimony. These were not enough, however, to provide for all their sons, and not all of them chose their friends and patrons wisely. Some members of the family became involved in rebellion and were forced into exile. Others prospered; Hugh of Grandmesnil, after a turbulent youth, became one of Duke William's most loyal vassals, took part in the conquest of England, and was rewarded with extensive fiefs centred on Leicester. But the somewhat ambiguous loyalties of members of the family have been characterized as loyal when the ducal or royal power was strong, rebellious when it was weak. Hugh's eldest son Ivo fell out of favour with William Rufus, and even his participation in the crusade did nothing to help him, for he and his brother Aubrey were two of the ignominious group of 'rope- walkers' who fled secretly by night from the siege of Antioch. Ivo never fully regained favour, and the honour of Leicester passed to the Beaumont family.

Another branch of the family likewise won and failed to hold great possessions in southern Italy. For a time they were among the highest nobility. William, another of Hugh's sons, left for Apulia between 1075 and 1080, at a good moment to join Guiscard's victorious campaigns. He fought well and was rewarded with the hand of Guiscard's daughter Mabel, who brought him fifteen castles, mostly in the Val di Crati. The family flourished until William attempted to win greater independence. His relations with the ducal family were often stormy; after a failed rebellion which forced him to seek refuge for a time in Byzantium, he returned to a diminished patrimony. His son Robert finally brought about the ruin of the family. Robert's quarrels with Duke Roger II in 1129 were important enough to deserve detailed treatment by the historian Alexander of Telese.[15] The issue was Roger's demand for increased military service, which Robert was unable or unwilling to provide; the final outcome was his banishment for ever to the lands of his family in Normandy. In that duchy at least the family continued to prosper. What remained of the family tradition in Italy and England was carried on by monks from Robert of Grandmesnil's abbey of Saint-Évroult in Apulia, Calabria and Sicily, and in England in the priory of Ware.

There were movements of churchmen no less than of knights. Cluny pioneered the way by sending out monks to teach its customs in new abbeys, as well as building up a network of dependent priories. Other

---

[15]   Alexander of Telese, I. 19, 20.

great abbeys such as Marmoutier and Bec-Hellouin also had their dependencies: conventual priories whose priors were appointed by the mother house, or daughter-houses much more loosely linked, which in time became independent. The practice of commemorative prayer was widespread; at first it was most conspicuous in the Cluniac houses, but the practice soon spread to independent Benedictine houses, including, in England, Durham and Thorney. The deaths of abbots and some other monks were recorded on prayer-rolls which were carried across Europe by monks: each house added the names of its own dead for whom prayers were requested. Saint-Évroult was associated in prayer with over eighty houses in Normandy, other parts of France, and in England; one was in Italy, at Venosa.[16] Mont-Saint-Michel had twenty-three spiritual fraternities in Normandy alone; Bec-Hellouin could count nine in England. The names of important lay benefactors were included in necrologies and sometimes added to the prayer rolls. Henry I's generosity to Cluny earned him a place in the commemoration of Cluniac houses all over Europe. Details of the number of trentals or other prayers to be recited and alms to be given to the poor varied; but all were open to mutual influence. Frequent intercession required many altars for the celebration of Mass, and this in turn brought about architectural changes. As with so much in the Norman world, however, the diversity was as great as the similarities.

Up to about the mid-twelfth century, when the influence of secular rulers on church appointments was strong, bishops and abbots were often chosen from Normans rather than from the local population. This practice was very widespread in England, where many members of the royal household were promoted to bishoprics, and Archbishop Lanfranc was influential in securing monks from reformed Norman houses to rule English abbeys. Such appointments were rarer in Italy. The choice of Guitmund, a holy monk from La-Croix-Saint-Leufroi as bishop in the Norman city of Aversa was unusual. Although the dukes and counts of Apulia and Sicily gradually replaced Greek with Latin bishops they sometimes looked to other provinces in France and northern Italy rather than to Normandy. The first four bishops appointed to the new sees created by Roger I in Sicily came from a variety of provinces; only Stephen was a Norman from Rouen, whereas Ansger of Catania was a Breton, Gerland of Agrigento a

---

[16] L. Delisle, *Rouleaux des morts* (Société de l'histoire de France, Paris, 1866); J. Laporte, 'Tableau des services obituaires assurés par les abbayes de Saint-Évroult et de Jumièges, *Revue Mabillon* (1956–7), 169–88.

Burgundian, and Roger of Syracuse a native of Provence.[17] Papal influence too began to be felt, and grew stronger. John, the monk of Bec-Hellouin brought in 1098 to rule the abbey of Telese, was made a cardinal two years later.

The creation of a kingdom in Sicily and the increase in public power and central administration both there and in the Anglo-Norman realm did not bring contacts and exchanges to an end; instead it changed their nature. The change has been broadly characterized as from one where the impetus came spontaneously through personal relations to one where intercourse between kingdoms and principalities was determined by regular diplomatic contacts, and solemn treaties increased in number and formality.[18] There was a certain amount of borrowing among the administrative officials; Thomas Brown, who had been employed in King Roger's secretariat, appears as an observer in the English exchequer. Roger II chose his great officers widely; his chancellors included the Englishman Robert of Selby and the Apulian Maio of Bari, while his greatest emir, George of Antioch, was Greek. Royal marriages sometimes brought in new households. When Margaret of Navarre, the wife of King William I was left a widow with an eight-year-old son, her great-uncle, Archbishop Rotrou of Rouen, sent some of his kinsmen and friends to help her in her task of regent.[19] They

Table 5　The French and Spanish relatives of Queen Margaret of Sicily

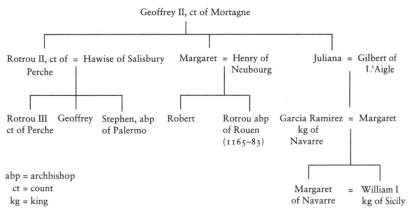

[17]　G. A. Loud, 'How "Norman"...?', 141–88.
[18]　E. M. Jamison, 'Alliance of England and Sicily in the second half of the twelfth century', in Jamison, *Studies*, 301–14.
[19]　See table 5.

included Stephen of Perche, who became chancellor of Sicily and archbishop of Palermo, and the peripatetic scholar, Peter of Blois. However a changed attitude was already evident in the opposition of some native churchmen to the 'foreign' ecclesiastics. Moreover, the circle of patronage widened after the marriage of Henry II's eldest daughter Matilda to Henry the Lion of Saxony, and his young daughter Joanna to William II of Sicily. Joanna brought her household with her, but she was widowed too soon to have any marked influence. And by that time, though movement across Europe was vigorous, there was little in the southern kingdom that was specifically Norman.

Peter of Blois, who came briefly to Sicily in mid-career, was one of the administrators living at a time when Norman family connections were only a limited part of the network of patronage and promotion extending across Europe. Even in the eleventh century Normandy itself had not been able to provide training for the sons of knightly families who chose neither to pursue a career of arms nor to enter a monastery. When William 'of Poitiers' turned away from his service as a knight to enter the Church he went to study in the schools of Poitiers before becoming a chaplain in the service of Duke William.[20] There were small schools attached to Norman cathedrals and secular colleges, but they catered chiefly for limited and local basic needs. The school established by Geoffrey of Montbray at Coutances was intended to provide training for the parochial clergy of his own diocese.[21] Odo of Bayeux sent his most promising clerks to study outside Normandy,[22] particularly in the schools of Liège, which in his day (like Laon in the time of Henry I) became a nursery for future bishops and abbots in England and Normandy.

Family contacts helped some men to travel far. One of these early travellers, who abandoned arms for study and the cloister, was Ralph son of Giroie, a kinsman of the Grandmesnil. He won renown, according to Orderic Vitalis, as a knight; perhaps his success on the battlefield provided the resources for the studies he later pursued, in grammar and dialectic, astronomy and music, in the schools of France, and at some stage in medicine at Salerno. He ended his life as a monk of Marmoutier, but was for a time seconded to Saint-Évroult to help the new abbot, his nephew Robert of Grandmesnil, and he was long remembered in the neighbourhood for his medical

---

[20] Orderic, ii. 78–9, 184–5, 258–61.
[21] Chibnall, 'Geoffroi de Montbray'.
[22] Orderic, iv. 118.

skill.[23] The one school of European importance to emerge in Normandy in the mid-eleventh century was the monastic school of Bec-Hellouin under Lanfranc. In Anselm's day it was said that Burgundians and Spaniards and others from far and near came to sit at his feet; by then, however, the abbey had become particularly renowned as a centre for spiritual devotion.[24]

Other schools rose in England, at Lincoln and particularly at Oxford, but their fame was to come later in the twelfth century. Up to the 1120s many ambitious scholars from the Anglo-Norman realm were drawn to Laon.[25] The most famous teacher in its schools was another Anselm; but some at least from the realm of the pragmatic Norman kings went to swell the crowds of students there for very practical reasons. For a time Adelard of Bath, one of the leading translators from Arabic, taught at Laon. He appears to have travelled along some familiar Norman routes, for he had visited southern Italy, where he dedicated a tract (*De eodem et diverso*) to William, bishop of Syracuse between about 1105 and 1115, and had then gone further east to Antioch for his studies.[26] A mathematician, he had translated Euclid's *Elements*, and become familiar with the abacus. At Laon he helped to train men with a future career in the English exchequer. His pupils may have included Thurkil, a royal clerk who wrote a short treatise on the abacus addressed to 'Simon of the rolls' a little before 1117. The thoroughly practical illustrations in Thurkil's treatise were chosen from English examples, such as '200 marks are to be divided among 2,500 hides, which is the total number of hides in Essex, as Hugh of Bocland says'.[27] So Arabic and Greek learning, partly at least acquired in the Norman principalities of southern Italy and Antioch, was taught in France and applied to the daily work of Henry I's exchequer in England.

Later in the twelfth century scholars hoping to equip themselves for high office in the Church and employment in the royal *curia*, whether in England or Sicily, tried to find the means to study in Paris or Bologna. A few took more unusual routes to promotion; such a one was Nicholas Brakespeare, the future pope Adrian IV.[28]

[23] Orderic, ii. 28–9, 74–6, 104.
[24] Orderic, ii, 294–7.
[25] R. W. Southern, 'The School of Paris and the School of Chartres', in *Renaissance and Renewal*, 115–17.
[26] Marie-Thérèse d'Alverny, 'Translations and translators', in *Renaissance and Renewal*, 421–62, at 440–1.
[27] C. H. Haskins, 'The abacus and the king's curia', *EHR*, 27 (1912), 101–6.
[28] R. W. Southern, 'Pope Adrian IV', in *Medieval Humanism and Other Studies* (Oxford, 1970), 234–50.

An Englishman who became a canon of St Ruf near Avignon, he made his name by being employed in the papal service; two years after being sent as a legate to Norway and Sweden he was elected pope. Robert Pullen took a more conventional route by way of Oxford and Paris to become a cardinal and papal chancellor. Others looked, not always with the success for which they hoped, to high office in England. Learning was sometimes thwarted by political involvement.

John of Salisbury, one of the most learned and witty scholars of his day, failed to rise as high as might have been expected. His career illustrates many aspects of the Norman world in the middle years of the twelfth century.[29] Born in England, probably into an ecclesiastical family, he grew up in Salisbury and Exeter, where he received in time a canonry though he was only intermittently resident. His years of study began in 1136 and were spent mainly, perhaps entirely, in Paris, where for some ten years he studied under the most famous masters and supported himself partly by teaching the children of nobles. On returning to England, he became employed in the household of Theobald, archbishop of Canterbury. His early letters were written for the archbishop; they show that though he had never studied at Bologna he had picked up enough practical knowledge of law to handle legal business.[30] It was on this business, particularly in appeal cases, that he travelled widely to Rome and throughout Italy. By the late 1150s he could claim in the *Metalogicon*, 'Ten times I have crossed the Alps since I first left England; twice have I journeyed to Apulia; I have done business often in the Roman court on behalf of my superiors and friends; I have also, on numerous occasions, travelled about Gaul as well as in England in connection with cases that have arisen.'[31] On one visit to Apulia he discussed questions of grammar with 'a Greek interpreter, who also knew the Latin language very well'.[32] On another occasion he heard Pope Eugenius III giving judgment in the divorce case of Count Hugh II of Molise.[33] In his one historical work, the *Historia Pontificalis*, which embodies his recollections of the years

[29] Christopher Brooke, 'John of Salisbury and his world', in *The World of John of Salisbury*, ed. Michael Wilks (Oxford, 1984), 1–20; David Luscombe, 'John of Salisbury in recent scholarship', ibid., 21–37.
[30] *The Letters of John of Salisbury*, I, ed. W. J. Millor and H. E. Butler, rev. C. N. L. Brooke; II, ed. W. J. Millor and C. N. L. Brooke (Oxford, OMT, 1979–86), I, pp. xix–xxii.
[31] John of Salisbury, *Metalogicon*, ed. C. C. J. Webb (Oxford, 1929); *The Metalogicon of John of Salisbury*, trans. Daniel D. McGarry (Berkeley and Los Angeles, 1955), III. prologue.
[32] *Metalogicon*, I. 15; (trans. McGarry, p. 44).
[33] *Historia Pontificalis*, ed. M. Chibnall (Oxford, OMT, 1986), 80–2, Appendix V, 99–100.

between 1148 and 1152, he showed knowledge of affairs in the principality of Antioch, gleaned from returning crusaders and from cases in the papal court.[34] So he was in touch, even without actually visiting, with some of the most distant outposts of Norman settlement.

The interruption to his career came after Theobald's death, when his resolute loyalty to Archbishop Thomas Becket forced him into exile for many years. These were spent, quietly enough, as a guest of his friend, Peter of Celle, abbot of Saint-Rémi in Reims. Even after Becket's death and his return to England he was never restored to Henry II's favour and was passed over for promotion to a bishopric. When towards the end of his life he was offered a bishopric it was not in any of Henry's lands, but in Chartres. That his promotion came from the king of France, through the intercession of a French bishop who was his friend and admirer, is perhaps not surprising given his previous career. His studies and friendship network and knowledge of affairs extended far beyond the purely Norman, into France and northern Italy (if not into Germany, whose inhabitants he regarded with distrust). He never called himself Norman; he had a strong attachment to his native England and he could even identify himself with Frenchmen, when, in writing from France, he contrasted the type represented by an English correspondent with 'us Frenchmen' (*nos Francos*).[35] This is typical of a time when many of the Normans settled in England were calling themselves English, and when the political structure of the Norman world was being reshaped. The schools were more international, the diplomatic contacts stronger, and the routes across Europe more frequently travelled than ever before. The Norman element remained, but it was gradually fading.

In many ways Latin learning progressively became more international. Some scholars wrote in a witty and allusive style for a small circle of readers; the most witty and esoteric of John of Salisbury's letters were addressed to particular individuals who would be able to appreciate them, and these were as likely to be French as Norman. Walter Map, canon of Lincoln and frequent attender in Henry II's court, produced in the work known as *Courtiers' Trifles* something of a rag-bag of popular legend, classical learning, shrewd comment on the devious ways of the royal court and pure gossip.[36] Unfinished, it was never circulated as a whole and the intended audience is a matter

[34] Ibid., 52–3, 61, 73.
[35] John of Salisbury, *Letters*, ii. no. 270, pp. 545–6.
[36] Walter Map, *De Nugis Curialium*, ed. M. R. James, rev. C. N. L. Brooke and R. A. B. Mynors (Oxford, OMT, 1983).

of guesswork. In the twentieth century it might have been privately printed for the members of a select dining-club. But the Latin history written in monasteries, the correspondence generated by cases of appeal all over Latin Christendom, the treatises of academic, theological or political interest, might be read anywhere in the schools, universities and courts of Europe. Simultaneously works written in the vernacular were having a more direct influence on lay readers. Those composed in Anglo-Norman are a clearer indication than the Latin writings of the surviving and changing culture of the Norman people.

Secular Norman society in the late eleventh and twelfth centuries was the seeding-ground of vernacular epic and romance. The Normans were great lovers of history – their history – and of the poetry celebrating the heroic lives of warriors comparable to their own heroes. Both were the principal entertainment of knights in the great halls. The twelfth-century romances were intended rather for recitation in the solars for the enjoyment of smaller groups composed chiefly of ladies.[37] The jongleurs who sang of past and more recent battles depended on patronage for their livelihood, and their *chansons de geste*, even when allegedly set in the time of Charlemagne, were adapted to suggest contemporary episodes. Occasionally the references went beyond suggestion to outright mis-statement, as when, in the *Chanson de Roland*, Charlemagne was credited with conquests in Apulia, Calabria, and even overseas in England:

> Merveilus hom est Charles
> Ki cunquist Puille et trestute Calabre,
> Vers Engleterre passat il la mer salse.

It has been argued plausibly if not incontrovertibly that the Baligant episode in some versions of the same *chanson* could have been based on the Illyrian campaigns of Robert Guiscard.[38]

Crusading armies were accompanied by some jongleurs, and others travelled in the courts of the east. The *Chanson d'Antioche* in the version of Richard le Pélerin, composed very shortly after the siege of Antioch, is the most historic of the known *chansons*.[39] Listeners were

---

[37]   M. Dominica Legge, *Anglo-Norman Literature and its Background* (Oxford, 1963).

[38]   *La Chanson de Roland*, ed. J. Bédier, 13th edn (Paris, n.d), lines 370–4; H. Grégoire and R. de Keyser, 'La chanson de Roland et Byzance', *Byzantion*, 14 (1939), 265–315; some corrections by M. de Bouard, *Bulletin de la Société des Antiquaires de Normandie*, 48 (1942), 608.

[39]   Lewis A. M. Sumberg, *La chanson d'Antioche* (Paris, 1968).

attuned to hear of superhuman acts of prowess; they may not have taken quite literally Godfrey de Bouillon's achievement in slicing a mailed pagan knight in two with one blow of his sword,[40] but they could applaud genuine triumphs and there are recognizable historical events in Richard's epic narrative. Later songs recounted with imaginative trimmings the trials and escapes of captives. The *Chanson des chétifs*, originating in Antioch, was probably inspired by the captivity of Bohemond and Joscelin of Courtney, count of Edessa, at Kharput.[41] Nearer home songs in the cycle of Guillaume d'Orange, the knight turned monk, could be linked to genuine battles in Spain. Jongleurs could help to soften the news of disasters by inventing campaigns of vengeance that existed only in the imagination. At times they may have succeeded in persuading knights in armies returning home that these events had really happened, with the result that the knights then related them to monk-historians, eager for news and ready to accept them as eye-witness accounts. Something of the kind seems to have induced Orderic Vitalis to soften his account of the disastrous battle of Fraga in 1137, and add a story of King Alfonso's revenge on the Saracens, whereas the unfortunate king had simply struggled home to die.[42]

Jongleurs naturally wished to please their patrons; patrons who were niggardly in their rewards ran the risk of being commemorated in a 'shameful song'.[43] Many patrons requested something more specific than a possible allusion in a *chanson de geste*. They wished for an account of their family history in the days of the first founder or (if the patrons were monastic) of a saint commemorated in their house. The 'ancestral romance' was often commissioned by men and women of the younger branches of Norman families settled in England and actively putting down their roots there. The practice spread to Scotland; the Old French *Roman de Fergus* may have been composed for the wedding of the great-grandson of the original Fergus of Galloway. A whole crop of such romances sprang up in England, including *Boeve de Hauntune*, *Waldef* and *Fouke le Fitzwarin*. They celebrated the founder of a family, whose prodigious and often imaginary deeds were interwoven with genuine historical and geographical material.[44]

[40] Orderic, v. 84 and n. 1.
[41] Orderic, vi. p. xxiii.
[42] Chibnall, *World of Orderic*, 203–7.
[43] Lambert of Ardres, *Historia comitum Ghisnensium*, MGH SS xxiv, 626–7.
[44] M. Dominica Legge, 'Some notes on the Roman de Fergus', *Transactions of the Dumfriesshire and Galloway Natural History and Antiquarian Society*, 27 (1948–9), 163–72.

The names and backgrounds of some of the authors suggest that either they or their families had emigrated from Normandy.[45] The name of Benediz l'Apostoiles, who wrote a *Voyage of St Brendan* first in Latin and then in French in the first decade of the twelfth century, indicates that he was a monk; it has been conjectured that he was professed at Bec-Hellouin and went to Westminster when Gilbert Crispin became its abbot. His patron was Queen Matilda; she was then holding her court at Westminster and surrounding herself, William of Malmesbury relates, with poets and musicians.[46] The French of Benediz was slightly archaic and eclectic, with a mixture of Norman, Occitan and possibly Italian words. Philippe de Thaon's name points to a family coming from the village of Thaon near to Caen, which boasts one of the purest early Romanesque churches in Normandy. In the course of a long life he too sought royal patronage, perhaps more hopefully than successfully; he dedicated works to three English queens (Matilda, Adeliza and Eleanor of Aquitaine) and to the empress Matilda. The contents of his books illustrate the wide interests of the ladies of the courts of Henry I and his wife and daughter. A *Cumpuz*, written probably in 1119, used the little treatise of the exchequer clerk Thurkil; he also wrote two French *Lapidaires*, a *Bestiaire*, and a *Livre de Sibylle*. There was evidently a popular, if limited, taste for books of marvels and prophecies, mixed with pseudo-science and moralizing; interest in the Sibylline prophecies was stimulated by contacts with southern Italy. Later writers in the second half of the twelfth century may have been second-generation settlers. The family of Hue de Rotelande, whose name derives from Rhuddlan, may have come to England in the entourage of Robert of Rhuddlan, a kinsman of the earl of Chester, Hugh of Avranches. However by the time Hue wrote he was settled on property near Hereford, and he chose to dedicate his romance *Prothelaus* to Gilbert fitz Baderon, lord of Monmouth, who died in 1191. The romances that he composed were of the same type as those popular in France such as the *Roman de Thebes* and the *Roman de Troie*. His *Ipomedon* and *Prothelaus* are disguised as tales of classical heroes, but are full of echoes of contemporary events in Sicily, Calabria and Apulia, and in France. The childless king, Meleager, in *Ipomedon*, can be seen as deriving from William II of Sicily, husband of Henry II's daughter

[45] M. Dominica Legge, 'L'influence littéraire de la cour d'Henri Beauclerc', in *Mélanges offerts à Rita Lejeune* (Gembloux, 1969), i. 34–5.
[46] WMGR, ii. 493–5; M. Dominica Legge, 'Les origines de l'Anglo-Normand littéraire', *Revue de lingustique romane*, 31 (1967), 44–54.

Plate 18   *Carving on the left-hand side of the tympanum of the façade of S. Maria della Strada, Matrice.*

Joanna; and the same poem includes a siege of Rouen with a direct reference to Henry's siege of Rouen in 1174.[47] It is characteristic of the easy familiarity of some aristocratic families with events ranging across the whole Norman world.

Traffic between the regions was always two-way. While historical characters in the Sicilian kingdom found their way into romances sung in the march of Wales, the heroes of French epics became sufficiently well known in southern Italy to be represented pictorially. There is convincing evidence that statues placed on the cathedral of Verona about 1150 represent Roland and Oliver; and stories from the *chansons* of Flooravent and Octavian, popular north of the Alps, have been identified in scenes carved on the façade of S. Maria della Strada at Matrice in the province of Molise (plate 18).[48]

The most visible expansion of Norman power and culture was in the castles and churches of the Norman conquerors. The Romanesque style developed in the duchy during its most creative period; it flour-

[47]   Walter Map, *De Nugis*, p. xxi; D. D. R. Owen, *Eleanor of Aquitaine Queen and Legend* (Oxford, 1993), 169–71.
[48]   E. M. Jamison, 'Notes on S. Maria della Strada at Matrice, its history and sculpture', in Jamison, *Studies*, 209–74, esp. 240–50 and plate X. 1.

ished and was gradually modified all over the Norman world for over a century and a half. From the time of the monastic and episcopal revival wealthy patrons built new churches in a magnificent style. Originally it owed much to Carolingian and Burgundian traditions, and embodied sufficient Roman elements to be christened 'romane' by nineteenth-century scholars. There were basic similarities of structure in the great churches everywhere. A Romanesque building has been described as 'the sum of an intricate network of subordinate parts, forming a balanced, harmonious whole'. A typical church consisted of 'a succession of bays, repeating a rhythmical pattern of piers and columns leading from the entrance to the altar, the large bays being surrounded by groups of smaller ones, with each bay crowned by a unit of vaulting... The sculpture and painting are closely linked to the architecture.'[49] Variations in plan were provided by different monastic customs. The activities of William of Dijon encouraged the appearance of Burgundian elements in the first Romanesque abbey churches at Bernay and Jumièges. In time Cluniac rituals helped to spread a type of plan with three or more semi-circular apses and ambulatories with radiating chapels.

Before 1066 the great churches of Normandy already embodied the Romanesque style. Enough survives at Bernay, Jumièges and Lessay (marvellously restored after the bombardment of 1944) to show its main characteristics and the grandeur of the new design (plate 19). Some traits, owing something to the influence of Robert of Jumièges, archbishop of Canterbury and later abbot of Jumièges, appeared in England in Edward the Confessor's abbey church at Westminster. But the main impact, both in England and reciprocally in Normandy, came after the conquest of 1066. The new wealth released for patronage by the enrichment of most of the leading magnates and bishops made possible the rebuilding of churches and castles on a scale unimaginable hitherto; and this, by providing constant employment for masons and craftsmen of all kinds, led to the development of greater technical skills. The best materials could be carried long distances; Caen stone was ferried to Canterbury and elsewhere; Tournai marble, already used occasionally in England, appeared at Winchester and further afield more frequently. Constant coming and going across the Channel led to cross-fertilization of every kind. So it is in England that most conspicuous growth and modification of the Romanesque

---

[49]   L. Musset, *Normandie romane*, i (Zodiaque, 1967); George Zarnecki, 'General introduction', *English Romanesque Art 1066–1200* (London, 1984), 15.

Plate 19   *Abbey church of Lessay (restored).*

architecture as created in Normandy took place. In the first two decades the Norman style appears at its purest, in (for example) the surviving parts of Lanfranc's cathedral at Canterbury, the north transept at Worcester and the nave of Winchester cathedral. After the initial impact, local influences began to introduce modifications, such as those visible in the west front at Ely, as well as in decoration. Norman builders employed local craftsmen, and they helped to perpetuate elements from Anglo-Saxon art in much more elaborate sculpture and decoration in both great cathedrals and modest parish churches. The same survival of native elements is apparent in manuscript decoration and wall-paintings. Moreover patrons and craftsmen were always open to new influences, particularly from Scandinavia and Spain, of the kind that appear in the elaborate carvings decorating the west door of Kilpeck church, and in the elaborate Romanesque

Plate 20 *Flavius Josephus, Jewish Antiquities, c.1130. Cambridge University Library, MS Dd.1.4. f.220 r, showing fully developed Romanesque initial. By permission of the Syndics of Cambridge University Library.*

Plate 21 *The south doorway of Kilpeck church. By courtesy of Ancient Art and Architecture.*

initials in many manuscripts (see plates 20 and 21). The eclecticism of Norman culture, however dominant the original Norman character-istics, was never more apparent than in the buildings of Anglo-Nor-man England.

Throughout the period church and castle attracted outside patron-age. Kings played their part in founding abbeys and building castles and palaces. At first much of William I's patronage went to churches in Normandy; chroniclers complained that he took away treasures from English abbeys to enrich foundations in Normandy. William at least founded one great abbey at Battle; and he and his sons led the way in building castles as centres of defence and attack, and also for residence. Stone towers replaced earlier wooden structures. William's Tower of London was a powerful defence, which also made provision for residence and government. Its chapel was one of the most spacious and beautiful of early castle chapels. Not many of the castles quickly erected all over England by king and magnates alike had the solidity of the Tower of London; but the majority were needed only for local protection. In some the great tower or *donjon* (of which one roofed

Plate 22 *Orford castle, Suffolk (Conway Library A86/5676).*
By courtesy of the Conway Library, Courtauld Institute of Art.

example still survives at Hedingham) was an important feature.
Within a generation more spacious and elegant living quarters were
provided. William Rufus took a practical interest in secular architecture; he built a spacious new hall at Westminster to provide for both
celebrations and business when his court met there. Some fragments of
sculpture show that it was decorated with secular themes, including
the storming of a castle. Both Henry I and his grandson Henry II
actively improved the amenities of the royal residences and hunting-
lodges in both England and Normandy (plate 22). Henry I built a new

Plate 23   *Petit Quevilly, chapel of St Julien – interior (Conway Library L45/33/19). By courtesy of the Conway Library, Courtauld Institute of Art.*

palace at Petit Quevilly, just across the Seine from Rouen, for more comfortable living than in the castle; and his grandson improved it. All that still survives is the lovely little chapel of St Julien, built in the 1160s by Henry II and his mother, the empress Matilda. It is remarkable for the high quality of its masonry, its carvings, and the recently restored paintings on its vaults, which are characteristic of English work of the time and may have been executed by English artists (see plates 23 and 24).[50]

Secular magnates and bishops were also active builders. Up to the middle of the twelfth century the magnate bishops were particularly important. In the first generation Odo of Bayeux, like Geoffrey of Coutances, was especially concerned with the building of his own cathedral in Normandy. The crypt and part of the nave of Bayeux survived the conflagration of 1106 and still remain as evidence of Odo's work. Another more controversial survival is the remarkable piece of embroidery, some seventy metres long, known as the Bayeux

[50]   Neil Stratford, 'The wall-paintings of the Petit-Quevilly', in *Medieval Art, Architecture and Archaeology at Rouen*, British Archaeological Association Conference Transactions, 12 (1993), ed. Jenny Stratford, 51–9.

Plate 24   *Petit Quevilly, chapel of St Julien – roof painting (restored)*
showing the Virgin and child (Conway Library L45/33/15). By
courtesy of the Conway Library, Courtauld Institute of Art.

Tapestry (plate 25).[51] Discussion of its purpose and making has filled
hundreds of publications; but through all the debate the association
with Odo and with Bayeux remains unshaken. The most plausible
interpretation is still that it was designed in part at least in Normandy,
executed in England (probably in Canterbury where there was a
distinguished school of needlework), and intended for display in the
cathedral of Bayeux, where the earliest references in the fifteenth
century describe it as being displayed. Whereas other pictorial friezes
of the period no longer exist, it has survived for over nine centuries, It
is equally important for the beauty and vigour of its design, the skill of
its execution, and the wealth of historical detail it contains. Odo's
castle building has left only a few traces; the huge motte at Dedding-
ton remains as visible evidence of the importance of his role in secular
government; and the traces of his park outside Canterbury of his
indulgence in the characteristic sports of the nobility.[52]

[51]   *The Bayeux Tapestry*, ed. F. M. Stenton (London, 1957); Shirley Ann Brown, *The
Bayeux Tapestry* (Woodbridge and Wolfeboro, 1988), lists publications up to 1988.
[52]   Tim Tatton-Brown, 'Recent fieldwork around Canterbury. 1. Three Deerparks',
Archaeologia Cantiana, 99 (1983), 115–19.

Plate 25   *The Bayeux Tapestry: Duke William enters Bayeux. By kind permission of the Society of Antiquaries of London.*

Plate 26   *Sherborne castle – beak-head ornament (Conway Library A84/ 1252). By courtesy of the Conway Library, Courtauld Institute of Art.*

A later magnate bishop was Henry I's servant, Roger bishop of Salisbury. William of Malmesbury wrote that he was 'unsurpassed within the recollection of our age for the pride he took in his buildings'. Unfortunately most of his work has perished; the great choir he built for the cathedral church at Sarum was abandoned in the next century when the cathedral was rebuilt at Salisbury; and very little survives from any of his castles. Sherborne has left the best remains (see plate 26). It was originally faced with ashlar blocks, so smooth, wrote the author of the *Gesta Stephani*, that the joins were invisible and the wall seemed to be a single block of stone. The ornate sophistication of some of the decoration attracted the notice of contemporaries. His castles were also spacious, designed for display and comfortable living.[53] Devizes was strong enough to survive some years of civil war in Stephen's reign, when the empress Matilda kept her court there and withstood all attacks. It is understandable that Henry of Huntingdon should have described it, with some exaggeration, as 'the most splendid castle in Europe'.

Perhaps the most outstanding example of a wealthy bishop able to draw on all the artistic resources of the Anglo-Norman world in its widest sense was Henry of Blois, bishop of Winchester, abbot of Glastonbury, and Cluniac monk. A great part of his wealth went to enrich the churches with which he was associated, and to improve the amenities of the see of Winchester by building palaces and castles. The Winchester annalist described him as 'unsurpassed in his care for enlarging and beautifying churches' (plate 27). Gerald of Wales was impressed both by his secular works, his sumptuous palaces, great lakes, ingenious water-works and marvellous collections of strange birds and animals, and by the rich vestments, great gold and silver jewelled crosses, altar vessels and illuminated books that even a king might envy, showered by him upon his cathedral church.[54] To those who were not beneficiaries he sometimes appeared predatory; he had a collector's eye for treasures, but was sometimes thwarted. The canons of Waltham held on firmly to a precious jewel in their miracle-working Holy Cross that he coveted; and Henry II recovered from him the arm of St James, which he had extorted from the empress

[53]   R. A. Stalley, 'A twelfth-century patron of architecture. A study of the buildings erected by Roger, bishop of Salisbury 1102–1139', *Journal of the British Archaeological Association*, 34 (1971), 62–83.
[54]   Giraldus Cambrensis, *Opera* (8 vols, RS, 1861–91), ed. J. S. Brewer, J. F. Dimock, G. F. Warner, VII, 45–6; *Annales Wintonienses*, in *Annales Monastici*, ed. H. R. Luard (5 vols, RS, 1864–9), II, 60.

Plate 27   *The Hospital of Holy Cross, Winchester, founded by Henry of Blois – crossing looking south-east into the choir (Conway Library A92/52). By courtesy of the Conway Library, Courtauld Institute of Art.*

Matilda after she brought it to England on her return from Germany. He was more successful in purchasing beautiful objects on his travels; on a visit to Rome he attracted the attention of John of Salisbury, and John commented with some amusement on this venerable bearded bishop, who went around buying up pagan statues.[55] Probably the treasures of Roman antiquity that he brought back to England account in part for the classical influence on some of the sculptures carved at Winchester in 1150-1. He had a keen eye for fine workmanship in whatever medium it appeared, whether in the sumptuous manuscript illustrations in the Winchester Bible, or the Romanesque enamelled plates of Mosan workmanship (now in the British

[55]   *Historia Pontificalis*, 79–80.

Museum) which may have been part of the decoration of a large altar cross.[56]

The career of Henry of Blois illustrates the way in which the original Norman inheritance could be enriched in the countries where the Normans settled, through generous patronage and the availability of skilled craftsmen and the finest materials. Some of these craftsmen were polymaths. One known by name, a certain Master Hugh who worked at Bury in the second quarter of the twelfth century, was an illuminator of manuscripts, a bronze caster and carver, and probably also a painter of murals. He worked on the Bury Bible, made bronze doors for the abbey, and carved the figures of St Mary and St John to stand beside a wooden crucifix. Some craftsmen formed small schools, which might work in different places. One artist known as 'Simon Master', who copied the recent commentary on Leviticus of Ralph of Flaix for abbot Simon of St Albans, was one of a group that also worked in France, at Troyes, as well as in England.[57] Such men assisted the transmission of new works of scholarship as well as the elaboration of styles.

As Norman settlement expanded, the direct influence of Normandy on art and architecture progressively weakened. The Romanesque style is clearly visible in parts of Scotland, for example in the churches of Dunfermline and Kelso, but to a much lesser extent in the castles of Ireland. Numerous mottes in Ireland testify to the rapid building of earth and timber fortifications during the first phase of settlement. The stone buildings and great towers that replaced some of them in the late twelfth and early thirteenth centuries tell a different story. In spite of appearances, they are not particularly strong as fortifications; the spacious and private buildings for the lord's residence, combined with all the trappings of defence that was little more than nominal, testify to a wish for status and comfortable living quarters as well as space for transacting business. This was characteristic of families who had settled and expected to stay. They built mostly on greenfield sites, and did not adapt older fortifications. Since many of these lords had had Angevin experience their great towers reflect French at least as much as English ideas.[58]

[56] G. Zarnecki, 'Henry of Blois as a patron of sculpture', in *Art and Patronage in the English Romanesque*, ed. Sarah Macready and F. H. Thompson (London, 1986), 159–72.
[57] Zarnecki, *English Romanesque Art*, pp. 23–4; Corpus Christi College Cambridge, MS 2 (see plate 3); Trinity Hall Cambridge, MS 2.
[58] T. E. McNeill, 'The great towers of early Irish castles', *ANS*, 12 (1990), 99–117.

Similarly in Italy and the Near East there was a weakening of direct Norman influence together with an openness to other cultures and a readiness to adapt to new ways of life. A few churches were clearly influenced by plans copied from Normandy and other parts of northern France. Aversa was one of the earliest cathedrals to imitate the northern style. According to William of Apulia, the Norman Rainulf Drengot fortified the city he had founded, and then sent to Normandy to invite rich and poor alike to settle there.[59] In 1053 the city became a bishopric; the cathedral was probably built at about the same time as the cathedral of Bayeux. The style of the stone vault was experimental, as in the north porch at Bayeux, though direct imitation was unlikely. The general plan with a semicircular apse and ambulatory with radiating chapels, however, corresponds to that of many churches in northern France, including the crypt of Rouen cathedral. It was to be repeated in the cathedral of Accerenza, and in the unfinished abbey church of Venosa.[60] In the early twelfth century Romanesque churches with more elaborate ornamentation were built elsewhere; they included S. Maria della Strada at Matrice and San Nicola of Bari, with its sculptured frieze of armoured knights above the north door. Cluniac influence is evident in the plan of Count Roger's abbey church at Mileto, as well as in a number of Sicilian churches. In Sicily, however, the Romanesque echoes are much fainter, and the cultural diversity of the kingdom profoundly modified the architectural style.

The strongest influences there came from Byzantium and the Arabic world, including Fatimid Egypt. From the time that Roger II was crowned as ruler of a realm with no royal tradition of its own, he worked to combine power with all the trappings of royalty he could bring together by borrowing from east and west alike. Architecture and decoration, ceremonial and regalia, all contributed to his magnificence. The chronicle of Romuald of Salerno described in enthusiastic detail how he built a very beautiful palace at Palermo with a wonderful stone floor and gilded roof, and had also built a palace at Favara; the building of the Ziza palace, however, was attributed by the chronicler to Roger's son King William.[61] In these palaces the 'solid ge-

---

[59] William of Apulia, i. lines 180–1.
[60] Mario d'Onofrio, 'Comparaison entre quelques édifices du style normand de l'Italie méridionale et du royaume de France au XIe et XIIe siècles', *Normands en Méditerranée*, 179–201.
[61] Romuald of Salerno, trans. G. A. Loud in *History of the Tyrants ... by 'Hugo Falcandus'*, 219–20.

Plate 28   *La Ziza, Palermo – general view from the east (Conway Library
466/67(31). By courtesy of the Conway Library, Courtauld Institute
of Art and Judith Herrin.*

ometry of the ground plan' and some additional features such as the
fountain inside the Ziza palace recall Egyptian buildings (see plates
28 and 29). The Arabic inscriptions and some of the scenes on the
painted ceiling in the Capella Palatina at Palermo show Arabic influence.[62] A stronger influence in the iconography and craftsmanship of
the cathedrals of Cefalù and Monreale came from Byzantium.
Whereas Roger I still wished to preserve some of the customs that
Norman monks had brought from his native Normandy, Roger II had
never been north of the Alps. He belonged to the Mediterranean
world, and his great wealth enabled him to purchase the best craftsmen and materials from the regions with which he had diplomatic and
commercial contacts. The teams of craftsmen who worked on the
mosaics of Cefalù, the Capella Palatina, and also on the Martorana
in Palermo came from Byzantium, probably from the imperial

[62]   Jeremy Johns, 'The Norman kings of Sicily and the Fatimid Caliphate', *ANS*, 15 (1993),
133–59.

Plate 29   *La Ziza, Palermo – the fountain court (Conway Library A66/63).*
By courtesy of the Conway Library, Courtauld Institute of Art
and T. J. Benton.

Plate 30   *Monreale cathedral – capital in cloister showing William II*
presenting his church to the Virgin Mary (Conway Library 603/65, 23a).
By courtesy of the Conway Library, Courtauld Institute of Art.

capital.[63] Echoes from the Anglo-Norman world are few; some figures and patterns that had become widespread have left traces in sculpture, notably in the figures carved on the capitals of the cloister of Monreale, and in the zig-zag ornamentation on the façade of Cefalù cathedral (plate 30). Transplanted cults of saints sometimes left traces; but the appearance of St Thomas of Canterbury in the mosaics of Monreale is exceptional. The rapid diffusion of his cult through France and into Italy made him an international as much as an English saint. The splendour of colour produced by the mosaics in Sicily does, however, help to convey to the eye something of the original impact of the Romanesque interiors of the great Norman churches in England when the wall-paintings were fresh and at their brightest. William of Malmesbury had emphasized colour when he described the total effect of the choir of Lanfranc's newly built cathedral in Canterbury:

> Nothing like it could be seen in England whether for the light of the glass windows, the gleaming of its marble pavements, or the many-coloured paintings which led the wandering eyes to the panelled ceiling above.[64]

The new Norman kingdom of Sicily exemplifies the changes in culture that had taken place in a hundred years as the Normans conquered across Europe and learnt to accept the styles and to use the riches of very different regions; but some basic traits remained just visible everywhere.

In Sicily the influence of the monarchy was particularly strong, but as in England wealthy patrons made their contribution to the beauty and variety of the new buildings. Roger II's great admiral (emir), George of Antioch, used the wealth gained in serving the king to found the impressive church of St Mary of the Admiral, known as the Martorana, in Palermo. He was an Orthodox Greek, born in Syria, who had lived in Egypt and in Al-Mahdiah. From the time he appeared in Sicily in 1114 he had a brilliant career; and by 1132–3 he had become emir of emirs; he was also a highly educated man and the centre of a literary circle. The church which he founded in Palermo has been called 'a major example of an architectural "collage", in which

---

[63] E. Kitzinger, 'The mosaics of St Mary's of the Admiral in Palermo', *Dumbarton Oaks Studies*, 36 (Washington, 1992); *idem, The Art of Byzantium and the Medieval West* (Bloomington and London, 1976).

[64] Cited Richard Gem, 'English Romanesque Architecture', in *English Romanesque Art*, 33.

Plate 31   *St Mary of the Admiral (La Martorana), Palermo – the campanile
(Conway Library 202/35 (11)). By courtesy of the Conway Library,
Courtauld Institute of Art.*

Byzantine concepts were juxtaposed with Islamic taste, executed by
local builders, and embellished by Byzantine mosaicists'.[65] His
church, unlike the Capella Palatina which glorified the monarchy,
was a monument to his devotion to the Virgin Mary (plate 31). Just
as Henry of Blois showed in his patronage something of his original
Cluniac monachism, Admiral George contributed a strong Greek
influence to the church he founded: it owed a little to the 'legacy of

[65]   Kitzinger, 'The mosaics of St Mary's', 66.

the Byzantine church of Daphni' near to Athens. Neither he nor his master, King Roger, had any direct contact with architecture north of the Alps; any Norman influence in Sicily was filtered more indirectly, by travelling scholars and diplomatic embassies. Moreover, by the time the dynasty founded by the Hauteville family came to an end, the Norman people in Sicily had become Sicilians.

10

The Normans after 1204

In 1204 Philip Augustus defeated his unruly vassal John and began the process of absorbing Normandy into the royal domain. The ties with England had been growing weaker for half a century. Some cross-channel families had already divided their estates so that one branch of the family retained the Norman patrimony and another settled in England.[1] Families on the frontiers of Normandy and France were also concentrating their interests in one region. The counts of Meulan, whose inheritance was partly in France, tended to use French dowries for their French marriages and Norman dowries for their Plantagenet matches; while the counts of Évreux gradually disposed of their lands in France.[2] The wars of Richard I and John against Philip Augustus were hard-fought, but after the French triumph there was suprisingly little resistance to French rule from the Normans in Normandy. Though many years were to pass before the kings of England accepted that the loss of Normandy was final, the existence of a true Norman people able to scatter colonies across western Europe and the Mediterranean lands had already come to an end. It was only in Normandy, their original home, that this multi-ethnic people settled down with a distinct, recognizable, but profoundly modified identity.

Throughout the thirteenth century the kings of France treated Normandy carefully, and in a different way from the other former Angevin provinces. The will and testament drawn up by Louis VIII in 1225 makes the distinction clear: 'Our son, who shall succeed us in the kingdom, shall have and hold the whole realm (*regnum*) of France and

---

[1]   L. Musset, 'Aux origines d'une classe dirigéante: les Tosny', *Francia*, 5 (1978 for 1977), 45–80.
[2]   Daniel Power, 'What did the frontier of Angevin Normandy comprise?', *ANS*, 17 (1995), 181–201.

the whole land (*terram*) of Normandy, with the exception of... the county of Anjou and Maine and the county of Poitou... which we divide between our other sons.' These other counties were provided as appanages for the younger princes; Normandy was to be governed directly, yet not simply as a part of the realm of France. It was allowed to keep its own identity under direct rule.[3] Separatism was not encouraged; no one was given the title of duke before John, duke of Normandy and heir to the throne, held it between 1332 and 1364. When Louis XI revived the title to make his brother Charles duke of Normandy in 1465 it was little more than a hollow sham. This may have helped to prevent the emergence of any separatist movement; it did not hinder the growth of a true regional identity within the French kingdom.

The strong and efficient administration that Normandy had enjoyed in the twelfth century was readily preserved by the French kings. Within this framework the Normans were able to claim and exercise certain financial and judicial privileges. The exchequer of Normandy was retained; 'according to the practice and customs of Normandy' (*ad usus et consuetudines Normanniae*) became a standard formula in royal writs. And Norman legal customs were respected. So, gradually, Norman finance and Norman law settled back into their traditional forms.[4] Many law-suits relating to finance were never taken from Rouen to Paris. At any time when these privileges seemed threatened the Normans defended them with passion, and petitioned the king for explicit confirmation of their rights. Throughout the later Middle Ages the Norman determination to preserve their particular character was embodied in the *Charte aux Normands*: a document often confirmed and sometimes respected. The *Charte aux Normands* was first confirmed in 1315 by Louis X, and although some of the concessions, notably the financial privileges, might be insubstantial, it was important to the Normans that they had some voice in the imposition of taxes, even if the amount to be collected remained the same.[5]

[3]   Charles T. Wood, '*Regnum Francie*: A problem in Capetian administrative usage', *Traditio*, 23 (1967), 117–47.

[4]   L. Musset, 'Quelques problèmes posés par l'annexion de la Normandie au domaine royal français', in *La France de Philippe Auguste. Le Temps des Mutations*, ed. R. H. Bautier (Paris, 1982), 291–307.

[5]   Thomas Basin, *Histoire de Louis XI*, ed. and trans. C. Samaran, i (Paris, 1963), 55–7; Philippe Contamine, 'The Norman "Nation" and the French "Nation" in the fourteenth and fifteenth centuries', in Bates and Curry, *England and Normandy*, 215–34; W. M. Ormrod, 'England, Normandy and the beginnings of the Hundred Years War 1259–1360', ibid., 197–213.

Although the Normans clung to and asserted their regional identity, there is little sign of any serious movement to break away from France and return to English rule. Even in the fifteenth century, when the victories of Henry V brought Normandy temporarily under English government and John, duke of Bedford, tried through moderation and concessions to win the hearts of the Normans, the people as a whole remained inflexibly loyal to the French monarchy. They wished to retain their individuality, but only within the kingdom of France. Some of the characteristics of the early Norman people survived, but in a form that harmonized with the immense political and cultural changes that had taken place.

Historical writing did not dry up completely. It was, however, no longer a celebration of the Norman people and their dukes. Much of the material in the *Chroniques de Normandie* was derived from earlier writers, going back to Dudo of Saint-Quentin, William of Jumièges and Wace. Material added from the thirteenth century onwards was either arid and factual or copied from Froissart and other writers until in the fifteenth century writers began to record contemporary events. By that time the Normans whom they praised were not conquering adventurers, but the loyal subjects of the French kings. After Henry V's claim to hold Normandy by hereditary right was inserted in the *Chroniques de Normandie*, the reply of King Charles firmly refuting his arguments was recorded in full.[6]

Of the fifteenth-century writers, Robert Blondel represented the most passionate Norman-French patriotism. His implacable hatred of the English may have been partly due to the loss of his family estates in the Cotentin in 1417 and his subsequent exile; the property was not restored until 1450, when the French reconquest of the province was completed. His most famous work, the *Reductio Normanniae*, described the wars with bitter feeling. Shot through with denunciation of the suffering, it included the idealized description of Normandy and its people that existed in tradition and memory:

Normandy was called Neustria by our earliest ancestors because of its natural fertility. Today it takes its name from those Normans who, sailing from Norway and fighting under Duke Rollo, won by the sword the coastal lands of Gaul and, gaining in time the whole province to its furthest boundaries, called it Normandy. It is bounded by the British Ocean to the east, an arm of the sea to the west, Gaul to the

---

[6] *Les Chroniques de Normandie (1223–1453)*, ed. A. Hellot (Rouen, 1881), chs VIII, IX.

south and the ocean to the north. It is a land which is very fruitful, with fertile fields, abundant pasture for flocks, rich woods and meadows, which support many kinds of wild animals and birds. It has an abundance of rivers and sea ports, is well-stocked with fruit-bearing trees, and is distinguished by noble towns protected by strong fortifications. Its metropolis is Rouen, an ancient town made powerful by its wealth and numerous population, which is situated on the river called Seine. Its people is strong and warlike, civilised in their customs, moderate in their speech, dutiful in their feelings, peaceful in their way of life, patient in toil, shrewd in the art of gaining wealth, devout in divine worship, reliable in paying tithe, obedient to their prelates, and devoted in their last moments to their supreme Lord.[7]

This is a picture of the Norman people which is traditional in form, but shows them remodelled as a wealthy, law-abiding and thriving regional people rather than world conquerors. Blondel was content to show the reconquest only up to the time that the whole territory of the province was won. The wealth of the land was traditional; there are echoes in his account of the words in which Orderic Vitalis had described Rouen, as it existed in the mind of the Normans of his day:

Rouen is a populous and wealthy city, thronged with merchants and a meeting-place of trade routes. A fair city set among murmuring streams and smiling meadows, abounding in fruit and fish and all manner of produce, it stands surrounded by hills and woods, strongly encircled by walls and ramparts and battlements, and fair to behold with its mansions and houses and churches.[8]

Indeed, in spite of war and ravaging, Normandy continued to be regarded as one of the wealthiest provinces of France. The eighteenth-century encyclopedists praised it unreservedly, as 'a beautiful and important province of France . . . one of the richest, the most fertile, and the most actively commercial of the kingdom . . . the province that has produced more brilliant and cultured people than any other.'[9]

Travellers from abroad might be more selective in their praise. Andrew Ducarel, visiting France in the mid-eighteenth century, noted the orchards everywhere, the woods well stocked with game, the corn of Upper Normandy and the pastures of Lower Normandy, the

[7] *Oeuvres de Robert Blondel, historien normand du XVᵉ siècle*, ed. A. Héron, ii (Rouen, 1891), 53–4.
[8] Orderic, iii. 36–7.
[9] Diderot et d'Alembert, *L'Encyclopédie ou dictionnaire raisonné* (Paris, 1757), 17 vols, 11, 228.

well-built houses and the populous towns. He observed, however, that the crops of many of the peasants were thin and poor, and blamed the heavy burdens imposed on them by secular landlords, adding that tenants on church lands fared better. This to some extent reflects the wealth of Normandy as seen from the viewpoint of government: the province was valued as an important source of taxes. It did not undermine the general picture, treasured by the Normans themselves for long after their reintegration in France, as a rich, gifted and shrewd people.[10]

Another fifteenth-century Norman historian, patriotic to France in spite of his hatred of Louis XI and his appreciation of the relatively orderly and strong government which England had given Normandy for a time, was Thomas Basin, bishop of Lisieux. He came of a prosperous merchant family from Caudebec-en-Caux, which managed by frequent movement to avoid the worst fighting after the English invasion of 1415. His studies began in Paris and Louvain, and led to a period of service at the papal court. When finally he returned to Normandy in 1441 to take up appointments in the chapter of Rouen and in the newly founded university of Caen, he was able to profit from the patronage of powerful ecclesiastics with English friends. On his appointment as bishop of Lisieux in 1447, he was even prepared to swear an oath of loyalty to King Henry VI for the temporalities of his see. This did not, however, prevent him from cherishing the traditions of the Normans, or from sympathizing with the loyalty many of the peasants continued to feel for the king of France all through the English wars. While appreciating good government wherever it could be found, and welcoming the restoration of the duchy by Charles VII, he was aware that the financial concessions made to the Normans by Louis XI amounted to nothing even before they were withdrawn. Picking up another trait traditionally attributed to the Normans – their litigiousness – and giving it a new twist, he blamed the lawyers for some at least of the oppressions suffered under King Louis.[11]

He commented on the number of secular lawyers 'some of whom were evil to the core, who continually incited the inhabitants of the land to embark on judicial suits and conflicts, to which they were all too prone'. They did this for their own profit, and although they were ignorant both of sacred learning and of secular law, by relying only on a few customs and practices which they continually distorted, they got

[10] Andrew C. Ducarel, *Anglo-Norman Antiquities Considered* (London, 1767), 94–5.
[11] Basin, *Louis XI*, 52–5.

a grip on the whole government of the province to such an extent that there was no one, not even a prelate or a noble of however great authority, who could escape from their power. They were, he insisted, solidly united; they controlled all the courts of justice in the province. This type of litigiousness, though perhaps reflecting earlier Norman characteristics, was a far cry from the eloquence and insistence on the maintenance of law and custom that had been so characteristic of the Normans at the height of their power.

Thomas Basin was a historian whose respect for tradition and custom led him to prefer the established feudal levies to the paid professional army then taking shape under Charles VII and Louis XI. Such a preference was to some extent in conflict with his admiration for the classical conception of history that he shared with Leonardo Bruni.[12] He was far less single-minded in his view of Normandy and its people than the passionate patriot, Robert Blondel. His ambivalence was characteristic of a time when both the French kingdom and the province of Normandy were moving into a new political framework. Normandy gradually emerged more firmly regional, more dependent on a thriving local economy and, above all, on its intellectual and cultural achievements and traditions for its survival as a separate entity. Its redefinition belongs particularly to the cultural changes from the later eighteenth century onwards, and is linked to the archaeological and antiquarian revivals of the nineteenth century.

Regional feeling began to be fostered from the mid-eighteenth century onwards by an interest in the past, at first largely academic. A small number of scholars browsing in monastic libraries and educated dilettanti travelling in Normandy became interested in the visible relics of the eleventh and twelfth centuries. Members of the newly refounded Society of Antiquaries in London began to investigate the links between England and Normandy. It was a communication read to the Antiquaries by the president, Charles, bishop of Carlisle, on the differences between Norman and Saxon architecture that led Andrew Ducarel to visit Normandy in 1752. His dedicatory letter to the bishop in his *Anglo-Norman Antiquities Considered*, published in 1767, described the impressions of his visit:

> When the English were obliged to forsake the province . . . they left
> behind them many valuable treasures. . . . These treasures are magnifi-

---

[12]   Mark Spencer, *Thomas Basin (1412–1490). The History of Charles VII and Louis XI* (Nieuwkoop, 1997), ch. III.

cent palaces, stately castles, beautiful churches, and sumptuous monasteries, together with a variety of monuments of every kind; all which
plainly evince the piety of their respective founders [see plate 32].[13]

His visit took in Caen, where he found the castle of William the
Conqueror 'much out of repair', Rouen, the abbey of Bec and Bayeux,
where he saw the 'historical tapestry preserved in the cathedral church
of Bayeux'. The tapestry had already attracted the attention of the
Benedictine monk Bernard de Montfauçon, who had described it in
his *Monuments de la Monarchie Française*. Ducarel added an appendix to his own book, containing 'a very accurate and circumstantial
description of the tapestry' by Smart Lethieullieur. It was, he said,
'hung up annually upon St John's day, and goes exactly round the nave
of the church, where it continues eight days'. According to him, the
clergy of the church knew only that it was hung up, and had no idea
that it related to Duke William.[14]

Plate 32   *Petit Quevilly, chapel of St Julien – interior before restoration.*
From J. S. Cotman, Architectural Antiquities of Normandy *(1822),*
plate XLIII. By permission of the Syndics of Cambridge
University Library.

[13]   Ducarel, *Anglo-Norman Antiquities*, Dedicatory letter.
[14]   Ibid., 79.

Within fifty years of his visit both the face of Normandy and the conception of its past had been transformed by the French Revolution and the Napoleonic wars. As in England after the dissolution of the monasteries, many monastic buildings were battered and abandoned, while the contents of their libraries were scattered. An outburst of national feeling under Napoleon threatened to engulf Normandy in French patriotism. Napoleon himself, who had studied the Bayeux Tapestry when he was contemplating the invasion of England, instructed the citizens of Bayeux 'to bring renewed zeal to the task of preserving this fragile relic, which records one of the most memorable deeds of the French nation, and likewise serves as a memorial to the enterprise and courage of their forefathers'.[15] Meanwhile romantic and nationalist movements in literature and history were slowly bringing back an interest in the study of peoples; it surfaced after the Restoration in the work of Auguste Thierry and – across the Channel – the novels of Sir Walter Scott. Behind the rhetoric, a serious local interest in the past showed itself in the foundation of learned societies. Most important in the revival of Norman awareness was the Société des Antiquaires de Normandie, founded in 1824 in Caen. The yearly volumes of *Mémoires*, supplemented from 1860 by the *Bulletins*, proved invaluable as an outlet for a wide range of archaeological, architectural and historical investigations into the past history of the Norman people and the duchy they had created out of the ruins of Neustria, as well as for their continuing traditions. The Norman love of history was being revived in a form appropriate to a different age.

Members of the Société des Antiquaires de Normandie included landed aristocrats and gentry, learned clergy, archivists teachers and politicians; there were intellectuals from other parts of France and from across the Channel. Sir Walter Scott, whose novels were greatly admired, contributed to the romantic element; Pugin continued the common interests in architecture that had helped to stimulate Ducarel and, in the early nineteenth century, J. S. Cotman. By leading archaeological investigations, collecting books in libraries, saving records from the makers of parchment lampshades, publishing chronicles and medieval romances, and petitioning local authorities against the demolition of ancient buildings, the members of the society helped to slow down the destruction and to preserve and interpret the surviving relics of the Norman past.

[15] Simone Bertrand, 'The history of the Tapestry', in *The Bayeux Tapestry*, ed. F. M. Stenton (London, 1957), 76–85, at 80–1.

Plate 33   *The church of Thaon, an early Romanesque church in*
Normandy (Conway Library). By courtesy of the Conway Library,
Courtauld Institute of Art.

From the first they aimed consciously at restoring the Norman
inheritance, not through the kind of elegant writing that had characterized earlier learned societies, but through fundamental research
into every aspect of Norman history and archaeology. As M. de
Caumont stated in his address to the society in January 1825, 'L'histoire du grand peuple dont nous descendons a été trop négligée; et,
riche en souvenirs glorieux, la Normandie a craint un moment de se
voir dépouiller des titres de sa gloire.'[16] Members were encouraged to
study the records and artefacts of their own regions, without neglecting the wider picture. Among the most enthusiastic of the antiquaries
was Charles Duhérissier de Gerville. Born in 1769, he belonged to an
aristocratic family from the region of Valognes in the Cotentin. His
law studies in Caen were interrupted by the Revolution, which forced
him into exile in 1793. After his return he settled on his estates,

[16]   *Mémoires de la Société des Antiquaires de Normandie*, 1 (1824), pt 1, pp. xlix–xlx.

collected manuscripts rescued from former monastic libraries, and devoted himself to the study of natural science and history. Acquaintance with England was a characteristic of this generation of scholars on both sides of the Channel; it encouraged comparison of architectural styles and exchange of documents. Both John Sell Cotman, who travelled in Normandy with his friend and patron Dawson Turner in the years 1817 to 1820, and Charles de Gerville realized from studying buildings of the Norman period that the architectural categories prevailing in England were inadequate. The term 'gothic' was being used to describe most medieval buildings later than the Saxon. When Cotman drew the 'monk's entrance' and the 'prior's entrance' to the Norman cathedral of Ely, he thought that, since the decoration was not gothic, it must be Saxon. At about the same time, in a letter to Auguste le Prévost, de Gerville suggested that an appropriate term for a style which echoed the characteristics of Roman architecture would be 'romane'; the word used by students to describe the language between low Latin and French (plate 33).[17] As 'romanesque' this description in time prevailed in England over the less satisfactory 'Norman', which was frequently used and persisted even into the twentieth century. Romanesque is more appropriate to the eclectic character of Norman culture.

Members of the Société des Antiquaires de Normandie were encouraged to study the buildings and archaeological remains in their own districts, and to collaborate in the publication of historical and literary works, from Dudo of Saint-Quentin and Wace to the vernacular epics and romances produced in Normandy. Caen, the home of the society, was to become an enduring centre of scholarly medieval studies and archaeology up to the present day.

De Gerville's own work, though appreciated in his day, was mostly ephemeral; but he had the great merit of being the first patron of Léopold Delisle (plate 34). The son of a local doctor from Valognes,[18] Delisle (1826–1910) came to know de Gerville while still a boy at school. From him he learnt palaeography by transcribing documents from the thirteenth-century cartulary of the abbey of Saint-Sauveur-le-Vicomte during the summer holidays. De Gerville also secured the contacts necessary to further Delisle's studies and (with Auguste Le

[17]   *MSAN*, 1 (1824), p. lxxxii; Musset, *Normandie Romane*, 10.
[18]   *Dictionnaire de Biographie Française*, 10 (1965), 842–4; D. Bates, 'Léopold Delisle (1826–1910)', in *Medieval Scholarship. Biographical Studies in the Formation of a Discipline*, I *History*, ed. Helen Damico and Joseph B. Zavadil (New York and London, 1995), 101–13.

Plate 34 *Léopold Delisle.*

Prévost) supported his entry into the recently founded École des Chartes. Although Delisle's formal studies in Paris were interrupted by the 1848 Revolution and a period of reorganization, he took advantage of the times when the École was closed to work at transcribing manuscripts in the Archives Nationales. Before he was thirty he had made two major contributions to Norman history. The first was his study of rural society and agriculture in medieval Normandy, which has stood the test of time. The second was his completion of Le Prévost's edition of the *Historia Ecclesiastica* of Orderic Vitalis, for which he wrote an introduction of remarkable range and penetration. Although he was persuaded by Benjamin Guérard to accept a post in the Bibliothèque Royale rather than one in the Norman departmental archives, and the remainder of his life was spent in Paris, his love of his native province remained undiminished. He was able to publish editions of Norman charters, the Chronicle of Robert of Torigny, and a history of Saint-Sauveur-le-Vicomte, and to prepare materials for an edition of the *Gesta Normannorum ducum* of William of Jumièges, whilst undertaking a fundamental reorganization of manuscripts in the Bibliothèque Impériale (later the Bibliothèque Nationale). It has been justly said that his work on the great Norman historians 'laid the foundations on which all modern work is based'.[19] At the end of his life, in his retirement, he returned to the history of Normandy by embarking on an edition of the charters of Henry II. It was at Chantilly, where he had an apartment as conservator of the Musée de Condé, that C. H. Haskins met him and found encouragement for his work on Norman charters. Though by no means the only scholar of importance in bringing to life the history and institutions of Normandy in the eleventh and twelfth centuries, he was undoubtedly the greatest.

Interest in the Norman past was not confined to specialists.[20] Among politicians, Guizot contributed a translation of Orderic's *Ecclesiastical History*. Napoleon's kinsman and emulater, Louis-Napoleon Bonaparte (later the Emperor Napoleon III) gave a subscription towards the erection of a statue of William the Conqueror in Falaise. The willingness of the local community to undertake, and largely finance, such a project is a symptom of a more widespread desire to commemorate past achievements. At a time when French national patriotism was inspiring huge popular paintings of scenes in early French history, regional patriotism was not slow to follow. In Normandy the conquest of England was the principal event to be remembered. The Battle of Hastings, the embarcation of Duke William for the Channel crossing, his entry into London and his death were among the subjects depicted for the museums of Rouen and Caen. In the nineteenth century commemorative festivals attracted the attention of a wider public. The 1911 millenary celebration of the traditional 'foundation' of Normandy by Rollo was the first of a series. Most commemorated episodes in Norman history, but in 1972 the participation of Normans in the conquest of Sicily was celebrated in the Cotentin, and a number of Sicilian bishops came to celebrate Mass in the little church of Hauteville-la-Guichard. Caen marked in

---

[19] Bates, 'Delisle', 106.
[20] Jean-Marie Levesque, 'Il mito normanno', in *I Normanni, popolo d'Europa 1030–1200*, ed. Mario d'Onofrio (Rome, 1994), 89–95.

1987 the ninth centenary of the death of William the Conqueror, with a series of lavish spectacles and processions. These, however, were rather more designed as tourists' attractions than as manifestations of enduring regional traditions. The preservation of the Norman myth and the investigation of the Norman achievement belonged to the heirs of Léopold Delisle, the Antiquaires de Normandie, and the centres of historical and archaeological study in the University of Caen.

Whereas the Breton people had their own language and some dominant ethnic elements that prolonged their identity in the French melting pot, the Normans had always taken pride in their mixed origins. They readily adopted the language of the people among whom they settled, and were noted for their readiness to intermarry. Their positive contribution to the legal customs of the region where they made their homeland helped to create a provincial identity that survived until the Revolution. Thereafter changes in administration and improvements in communications gradually undermined their separate customs. The pull of Paris was strong in culture no less than in economic life. If artists like Monet, who made their name in Paris, returned on visits to make the churches of Rouen and the beaches of Étretat familiar in Parisian galleries, more and more gifted young Normans left their native province for good. Politically the Normans of the eleventh and twelfth centuries had made their contribution to the laws and governmental structures of several national states, which by the late twentieth century were learning to adapt themselves to a changing political climate and a global economy. They continued to exist in history and memory, and could be commemorated in London, Rouen, Palermo, or Rome in great exhibitions which were a continuing reminder of their achievements. A modern historian, writing about the 1994 Rome exhibition of the Normans as a European people, summed up the present-day interest in the Normans.[21] He suggested that the recreation of a historical period, rich in concrete facts and major socio-cultural developments, could help to show that a people, now absorbed into several different nations, had been a significant common element of true value in the formation of a new European consciousness.

[21]   Jean-Yves Marin, 'La coscienza normanna oggi', in *I Normanni*, 373.

Select Bibliography

Abulafia, David, 'The Norman Kingdom of Africa and the Norman expeditions to Majorca and the Muslim Mediterranean', *ANS*, 7 (1985), 26–49.

Alexander of Telese: *Alexandri Telesini abbatis ystoria Rogerii regis Sicilie Calabrie atque Apulie*, ed. L. de Nova, commentary D. Clementi, Fonti per la storia d'Italia (Rome, 1991).

Alexiad: *The Alexiad of Anna Comnena*, trans. R. A. Sewter (Harmondsworth, 1969).

Amatus (Aimé) of Montecassino, *Storia di Normanni di Amato di Montecassino*, ed. V. de Bartholomeis, Fonti per la storia d'Italia (Rome, 1935).

Barlow, Frank (ed.), *The 'Carmen de Hastingae Proelio' of Guy Bishop of Amiens* (Oxford, OMT, 1999).

Barrow, G. W. S., *The Anglo-Norman Era in Scottish History* (Oxford, 1980).

Basin, Thomas, *Histoire de Louis XI*, ed. and trans. C. Samaran (Paris, 1963).

Bates, David, *Normandy before 1066* (London and New York, 1982).

Bates, David and Curry, Anne (eds), *England and Normandy in the Middle Ages* (London and Rio Grande, 1994).

Bayeux Tapestry: *The Bayeux Tapestry*, ed. F. M. Stenton (London, 1951).

Baylé, Maylis (ed.), *L'Architecture Normande au Moyen Age*, 2 vols (Caen, 1997).

Beech, George, 'A Norman adventurer in the East: Richard of Salerno 1097–1112', *ANS*, 15 (1993), 25–40.

Bennett, Matthew, 'Norman naval activity in the Mediterranean c.1060–c. 1108', *ANS*, 15 (1993), 41–58.

Benoît: *Chronique des ducs de Normandie par Benoît*, ed. C. Fahlin, 2 vols (Uppsala, 1951–7).

Bisson, T. N. (ed.), *Cultures of Power: Lordship, Status and Process in the Twelfth Century* (Philadelphia, 1995).

Blondel, Robert, *Oeuvres de Robert Blondel, historien normand du XVe siécle*, ed. A. Heron (Rouen, 1981).

Brown, R. Allen, *The Normans* (London, 1984).

Brown, R. Allen, *Castles from the Air* (Cambridge, 1989).

Brown, R. A., Colvin, H. M. and Taylor, A. J., *The King's Works*, I (London, 1984).

Bouet, Pierre and Neveux, François (eds), *Les Normands en Méditerranée* (Caen, 1994).

Bouet, Pierre and Neveux, François (eds), *Les évêques normands du XIe siècle* (Caen, 1995).

Byock, Jesse L., *Medieval Iceland: Society, Sagas and Power* (Enfield Lock, 1993).

Cahen, C., *La Syrie du Nord* (Paris, 1940).

Campbell, James, *The Anglo-Saxons* (London, 1982).

Campbell, James, *The Anglo-Saxon State* (Hambledon Press, 2000).

Catalogus Baronum, ed. E. M. Jamison, Fonti per la storia d'Italia (Rome, 1972).

Chibnall, M., *The World of Orderic Vitalis* (Oxford, 1984; repr. Woodbridge, 1996).

Chibnall, M., *Anglo-Norman England 1066–1166* (Oxford, 1986).

Chibnall, M., *The Debate on the Norman Conquest* (Manchester, 1999).

Contamine, Philippe, 'The Norman "Nation" and the French "Nation" in the fourteenth and fifteenth centuries', in Bates and Curry (eds), *England and Normandy*.

Couronnement (Le) de Louis: Chanson de geste du XIIe siècle, ed. E. Langlois, Les classiques français du Moyen Age (Paris, 1920).

Davies, R. R., *Conquest, Coexistence and Change: Wales, 1062–1415* (Oxford, 1987).

Davis, R. H. C., *The Normans and their Myth* (London, 1976).

Davis, R. H. C., *The Medieval War Horse: Origin, Development and Re-development* (London, 1989).

Davis, R. H. C., *From Alfred the Great to Stephen* (London and Rio Grande, 1991).

Decaens, Joseph, 'Le patrimoine des Grandmesnil en Normandie, en Italie et en Angleterre', in Bouet and Neveux (eds), *Les Normands en Méditerranée*, 123–40.

Dolley, M., *The Norman Conquest and the English Coinage* (London, 1966).

Douglas, D. C., *William the Conqueror* (London, 1964).

Douglas, D. C., *The Norman Achievement* (London, 1969).

Ducarel, Andrew C., *Anglo-Norman Antiquities Considered* (London, 1976).

Dudo of Saint-Quentin, *De moribus et actis primorum Normanniae ducum*, ed. Jules Lair (*MSAN*, Caen, 1865); trans. Eric Christiansen, *History of the Normans* (Woodbridge, 1998).

English Romanesque Art 1066–1200. Catalogue of the 1984 Exhibition at the Hayward Gallery, London (London, 1984).

Fauroux, Marie (ed.), *Recueil des actes des ducs de Normandie de 911 à 1066* (*MSAN* 36, Caen, 1961).

Fedden, Robin and Thomson, John, *Crusader Castles* (London, 1957).

Fernie, E. C., 'The effect of the Conquest on Norman architectural patronage', *ANS*, 9 (1987), 71–85.

Flanagan, M. T., 'Strategies of lordship in pre-Norman and post-Norman Leinster', *ANS*, 20 (1998), 107–26.

Fleming, Robin, *Kings and Lords in Conquest England* (Cambridge, 1991).

Fleming, Robin, *Domesday Book and the Law* (Cambridge, 1998).

Fleming, Robin, 'Picturesque history and the Medieval in nineteenth-century America', *American Historical Review*, 100 (1995), 1061–14.

Frame, Robin, *Colonial Ireland: Feudal Power in a Gaelic World* (London and New York, 1997).

Frappier, Jean, *Les Chansons de geste du cycle de Guillaume d'Orange*, 3 vols (Paris, 1955–83).

Fulk of Benevento: *Falconis Beneventani Chronicon*, ed. Del Re Cronisti e scrittori sincroni editi e inediti, I (Naples, 1845).

Gaillou, P. and Jones, M., *The Bretons* (Oxford, 1991).

Gaimar, Geffrei, *L'Estoire des Engleis*, Anglo-Norman Text Society, 14–16 (Oxford, 1960).

Gem, Richard, 'English Romanesque architecture', in *English Romanesque Art*, 27–40.

Gillingham, John, *The English in the Twelfth Century* (Woodbridge, 1999).

Gillingham, John, 'William the Bastard at war', in *Studies in Medieval History presented to R. Allen Brown*, ed. C. Harper-Bill, C. Holdsworth and J. L. Nelson (Woodbridge, 1989).

GND: The 'Gesta normannorum ducum' of William of Jumièges, Orderic Vitalis and Robert of Torigni, ed. E. M. C. van Houts, 2 vols (Oxford, OMT, 1992–5).

Golding, Brian, *Conquest and Colonisation: The Normans in Britain* (Oxford, 1994).

Green, Judith, *The Aristocracy of Norman England* (Cambridge, 1997).

Hamilton, Bernard, *The Latin Church in the Crusader States: The Secular Church* (London, 1980).

Harper-Bill, C., 'Herluin, abbot of Bec and his biographer', *Studies in Church History*, 15, ed. Derek Baker (Oxford, 1978), 15–25.

Haskins, C. H., *The Normans in European History* (Boston and New York, 1915).

Haskins, C. H., *Norman Institutions* (Cambridge, Mass., 1925).

Henry, Archdeacon of Huntingdon, Historia Anglorum, ed. Diana Greenway (Oxford, OMT, 1996).

Hiley, David, 'Quanto c'è di normanno nei tropari Siculo-Normanni?', *Rivista italiana di musicologia*, 18 (1981), 3–28.

Holt, J. C. (ed.), *Domesday Studies* (Woodbridge, 1987).

Holt, J. C., *Colonial England, 1066–1232* (London and Rio Grande, 1997).

Houben, Hubert, 'Roberto II Guiscardo e il monachesimo', *Benedictina*, 32 (1985), 495–520.

Hugo Falcandus: *The History of the Tyrants of Sicily by Hugo Falcandus 1154–69*, ed. and trans. T. Wiedemann and G. A. Loud (Manchester, 1998).

I Normanni, popolo d'Europa 1030–1200, ed. Mario d'Onofrio (Rome, 1994).

Jamison, Evelyn M., *Admiral Eugenius of Sicily* (London, 1957).

Jamison, Evelyn M., *Studies in the History of Medieval Sicily and South Italy*, ed. Dione Clementi and Theo Kölzer (Aalen, 1992).

John of Salisbury: *The Historia Pontificalis of John of Salisbury*, ed. M. Chibnall (Oxford, OMT, 1986).

John of Salisbury: *The Letters of John of Salisbury*, I, ed. W. J. Millor and H. E. Butler, rev. C. N. L. Brooke; II, ed. W. J. Millor and C. N. L. Brooke (Oxford, OMT, 1979–86).

John of Salisbury: *The 'Metalogicon' of John of Salisbury*, trans. D. D. M. McGarry (Berkeley and Los Angeles, 1953).

Johns, Jeremy, 'The Norman kings of Sicily and the Fatimid caliphate', *ANS*, 15 (1993), 133–59.

Kitzinger, E., 'The mosaics of St Mary's of the Admiral in Palermo', *Dumbarton Oaks Studies*, 36 (Washington, 1992).

Knowles, David, *The Monastic Order in England*, 2nd edn (Cambridge, 1966).

Leges Henrici Primi, ed. L. J. Downer (Oxford, 1972).

Legge, Dominica, *Anglo-Norman Literature and its Background* (Oxford, 1963).

Le Patourel, John, *The Norman Empire* (Oxford, 1976).

Loud, G. A., 'How "Norman" was the Norman conquest of southern Italy?', *Nottingham Medieval Studies*, 25 (1981).

Loud, G. A., 'The genesis and context of the Chronicle of Falco of Benevento', *ANS*, 15 (1993), 177–98.

Loud, G. A., 'A Lombard Abbey in a Norman world: St Sophia, Benevento, 1050–1200', *ANS*, 19 (1997), 273–306.

Louis, René, 'Les ducs de Normandie dans les chansons de geste', *Byzantion*, 28 (1958), 391–419.

Malaterra: *Gaufridi Malaterra, 'De rebus gestis Rogerii Calabriae et Siciliae comitis et Roberti Guiscardi fratris eius'*, ed. E. Pontieri, *Rerum Italicarum Scriptores* V^i (Bologna, 1928).

Martin, J. M., *La Pouille du VIe au XIIe siècle*, Collection de l'École Française de Rome (1956).

Matthew, Donald, *The Norman Kingdom of Sicily* (Cambridge, 1992).

McCrank, L. J., *Medieval Frontier History in New Catalonia* (Variorum Studies Series, London, 1996).

McNeill, T. E., *Castles in Ireland: Feudal Power in a Gaelic World* (London and New York, 1997).

Ménager, L.-R., *Hommes et institutions de l'Italie normande* (Variorum Studies Series, London, 1981).

Musset, Lucien, *Angleterre Romane* (Zodiaque, n.d.).

Musset, Lucien, *Normandie Romane*, 2 vols (Zodiaque, 1967–74).

Musset, Lucien, 'Naissance de la Normandie, in *Histoire de Normandie*, ed. M. de Bouard (Toulouse, 1970).

O'Brien, Bruce, *God's Peace and King's Peace: The Laws of Edward the Confessor* (Philadelphia, 1999).

Orderic: *The Ecclesiastical History of Orderic Vitalis*, ed. M. Chibnall, 6 vols (Oxford, OMT, 1969–80).

Pollock, F. and Maitland, F. W., *The History of English Law before the Time of Edward I*, 2nd edn, 2 vols (Cambridge, 1968).

Potts, Cassandra, *Monastic Revival and Regional Identity in Early Normandy* (Woodbridge, 1997).

Renaissance and Renewal in the Twelfth Century, ed. R. L. Benson and Giles Constable (Cambridge, Mass., 1982).

Ridyard, S. J., '*Condigna Veneratio*: post-Conquest attitudes to the saints of the Anglo-Saxons', *ANS*, 9 (1987), 179–206.

Rowlands, I. A., 'Aspects of the Norman settlement in Dyfed', *ANS*, 3 (1981), 142–57.

Searle, Eleanor, *Predatory Kinship and the Creation of Norman Power 840–1066* (Berkeley, 1988).

van Houts, E. M. C., *History and Family Traditions in England and the Continent 1000–1200* (Variorum Collected Studies Series, London, 2000); contains 'Scandinavian influence on Norman literature of the eleventh century'; 'Historiography and hagiography at Saint-Wandrille'; 'The ship-list of William the Conqueror'; 'The adaptation of *Gesta Normannorum Ducum* by Wace and Benoît'.

Wace: *Le Roman de Rou de Wace*, ed. A. J. Holden, 3 vols (Société des anciens textes français, Paris 1970–3).

Waley, D. P., 'Combined operations in Sicily, AD 1060–78', *Papers of the British School at Rome*, 22 (1954), 185–205.

Walker, David, *The Normans in Britain* (Oxford, 1995).

Walter Map, *De Nugis Curialium*, ed. M. R. James, rev. C. N. L. Brooke and R. A. B. Mynors (Oxford, OMT, 1983).

Werner, K. F., 'Quelques observations au sujet des débuts du duché de Normandie', in *Droit privé et institutions régionales: Études historiques offertes à Jean Yver* (Paris, 1976), 692–709.

William of Apulia: *Guillaume de Pouille, 'La geste de Robert Guiscard'*, ed. M. Mathieu, Istituto siciliano di studi bizantini e neoellenici, Testi e Monumenti, 4 (Palermo, 1961).

William of Malmesbury, *De gestis pontificum Anglorum libri quinque*, ed. N. E. S. A. Hamilton (RS, London, 1870).

William of Malmesbury, *De gestis regum Anglorum libri quinque*, ed. W. Stubbs, 2 vols (RS, London, 1887–9).

William of Poitiers: *The 'Gesta Guillelmi of William of Poitiers'*, ed. R. H. C. Davis and M. Chibnall (Oxford, OMT, 1998).

Williams, Ann, *The English and the Norman Conquest* (Woodbridge, 1995).

Wormald, Patrick, *The Making of English Law: King Alfred to the Norman Conquest* (Oxford, 1999).

Yewdale, R. B., *Bohemond I, Prince of Antioch* (Princeton, 1924).

Yver, Jean, 'Les châteaux forts en Normandie jusqu'au milieu du XIIᵉ siècle', *BSAN*, 53 (1957 for 1955–6), 28–115, 604–9.

Yver, Jean, *Égalité entre héritiers et exclusion des enfants dotés* (Paris, 1966).

Zarnecki, George, 'General introduction', in *English Romanesque Art 1066–1200* (London, 1984), 15–26.

Index

abacus, 137
Accerenza, cathedral, 155
acculturation, 32, 54, 70, 88
Adelaide, wife of Count Roger I of
  Sicily, 83
Adelard of Bath, 137
Adeliza, wife of King Henry I, 142
Adrian IV (Nicholas Brakespeare),
  pope, 87, 137–8
Aeneas the Trojan, 17
Africa, 94, 102–3
Ailred of Rievaulx, 112
Alan, son of Geoffrey duke of
  Brittany, 22
Alan III of Richmond, count, 110
Alençon (Orne), castle, 29–30
Alexander I, king of Scots, 69
Alexander of Telese, abbot and
  historian, 83, 86, 120–2
Alexius I Comnenus, emperor, 92,
  96, 97, 116, 119
Alfonso (the Battler), king of
  Aragon, 141
Amalfi, 76, 86, 91, 95
Amatus of Monte Cassino, 76,
  80, 119
Anacletus II, pope, 85, 86
Angers (Maine-et-Loire), 10
'Angevin empire', 64
Anglo-Norman, use of term; 68, 111;
  aristocracy in Ireland, 70, 72

Anglo-Saxons, art, 145; *and see*
  architecture; customs
Anglo-Saxon Chronicle, 10, 113
Anjou, 31; counts of, 29; *and
  see* Fulk, Geoffrey
Anna Comnena, her *Alexiad*,
  78, 122–3
annals, Frankish, 10, 11; Norman,
  16; Italian, 83, 120
Anselm (St), abbot of Bec-Hellouin,
  archbishop of Canterbury, 26, 55,
  58, 68, 126, 137
Anselm of Laon, 137
Antioch, 83, 96; church in, 98;
  patriarch, 98; principality, 97–100,
  103, 125, 131, 137, 139, 141;
  siege, 96, 133, 140
appanages, 162
Apulia, 75, 77, 78, 79, 86, 90, 91,
  95, 113, 115, 129, 133, 138, 140
Aquitaine, men from, 109
Arabic, translations, 137; influence in
  Sicily, 156
archers, 26, 41
architecture, Anglo-Saxon, 166, 170;
  Romanesque, 170; *and see*
  Burgundians; Cluny
Armorica, 5
armour, 27
Arnold, count of Flanders, 13
Arnulf of Montgomery, 70

The Normans

Marjorie Chibnall

Copyright © Marjorie Chibnall 2000

The right of Marjorie Chibnall to be identified as author of this work has been
asserted in accordance with the Copyright, Designs and Patents Act 1988.

First published 2000

2 4 6 8 10 9 7 5 3 1

Blackwell Publishers Ltd
108 Cowley Road
Oxford OX4 1JF
UK

Blackwell Publishers Inc.
350 Main Street
Malden, Massachusetts 02148
USA

British Library Cataloguing in Publication Data

A CIP catalogue record for this book is available from the British Library.

Library of Congress Cataloging-in-Publication Data

Chibnall, Marjorie.
The Normans/Marjorie Chibnall.
p. cm. — (The peoples of Europe)
Includes bibliographical references and index.
ISBN 0–631–18671–9 (alk. paper)
1. Normans—History.   2. Europe—History—476–1492.
3. Normandy (France)—History—To 1515.
I. Title.   II. Series.

D148.C48 2001
909′.04395—dc21   00–033665

Typeset in 10.5 on 12.5pt Sabon
by Kolam Information Services Pvt. Ltd, Pondicherry, India
Printed in Great Britain by MPG Books Ltd, Bodmin, Cornwall

This book is printed on acid-free paper